LADS - The Eighties

First Published by Lads Books in the UK 2009

ISBN 13: 978-0-9559769-1-9

www.ladsbooks.co.uk

I dedicate this book to Emma, Freemo junior's daughter, who was born in this decade on 6th August 1986. She was just fifteen when her Dad died suddenly. She was nineteen when her Mum died. I'm very proud of the way you've grown up, Em. Sorry about the language!

Freemo

CONTENTS

..... The Lads at the start of the eighties

1. Stoke City Away – Graveyard Shenanigans

2. Wolves at Hillsborough – FA Cup Semi Final

3. Manchester City – The Centenary Cup Finals

4. TTHLSHGBCC – A new institution

5. Anderlecht Away – UEFA Cup Final first leg

6. Everton Away – Arses on fire

7. Sunderland Away – Full of Beans

8. Halifax Away – Flat caps and TV stardom

9. The Italian Job – A holiday in Cattolica

10. Coventry City – F A Cup Final woes

11. Freemo's Second Wedding – Hollins creates havoc

12. Middlesbrough Away – The Empire strikes back

13. Palace Away – A Bit of a Rumble

14. Q.P.R. Away – Kidnapping the Pole

The Lads Nowadays.....

15. A complete record of results during the Eighties

THE LADS AT THE START OF THE EIGHTIES

This book continues telling the story about the lives, loves, events, passions and adventures surrounding four hard drinking, football-mad men in their thirties as they follow their beloved football team – Tottenham Hotspur. 'The Lads' live in the Midlands city of Worcester in the 1980s and home games are a 200 mile plus round trip by car or train. The book is based entirely on true stories….

Worcester in the 1980s had not changed much since the previous decade – a few more areas of modern, boxy housing to fill in the gaps between the main roads out of town; a bit of town centre pedestrianisation and tree planting; a few clubs closed and a few new ones opened, but nothing much.

At the start of the decade, Freemo works at a large catalogue company as a computer programmer. He is beginning to impress by 1980, after a faltering start where he got pissed for three months as his fiancée Helen stepped out with a guy in pink trousers. Now he was responsible for making sure all the programmes ran successfully overnight so things were all ready for the office workers the next morning. Everyone had lost count of the number of times he had to be picked up because he was too pissed to drive to work in the middle of the night, but he always managed to get it sorted out (and got a lie in next morning for his trouble).

Hollins is now working for Berrows newspapers – publishers of the oldest newspaper in the land (Berrows Journal). Nobody – even he it seems – is quite sure of what he does there, but the pay is OK and the social life is great. They're flexible about time off for football too and turn a blind eye to certain necessary sickies for big games, so Pete was in no rush to do anything else, it seemed.

Smiffy is still doing something or other in the printing trade. It involves books and binding and lots of technical things that the others didn't understand, but they pretended anyhow. By 1980 he was divorced from his first wife, Julie and had met Lesley – his new fiancée – at work. Seems she did something or other in the printing trade too.

Spence was with Pauline and not going to quite so many games. Glenn was soliciting and they had lost touch. Cowboy was on the black stuff (the roads, not the Moroccan). Crowbar worked with Hollins at Berrows – for all the same reasons. Buzz still works at the same catalogue company as Freemo. Shaun had moved to Mallorca, via a stint in New Zealand – he was a brilliant ceramic artist but had had enough of that and first bought a hotel, then some shops on the Spanish island. Freemo jnr. had left school and home and was drifting around – most of the time 'between jobs'. Steve C. from Evesham (did he get a mention in the first book?) was out of the game – he had first been mugged by his fellow Spurs fans and so changed to Millwall. Apparently he also got nicked for stealing women's underwear from washing lines. He still worked at the pork pie factory and still wore a dog collar (the dog kind, not the religious version), but only the Evesham lads still see him round and about – or so Stevesham and Sensible Keith say…

CHAPTER ONE

SHENANIGANS IN THE GRAVEYARD
STOKE CITY AWAY
(4/10/1980)

Only a few of the lads made the trip this particular week. Stoke wasn't the most exciting place in the world – a small, grimy industrial city made up of a collection of small, grimy pottery towns. Spartan pubs. A long walk from the station to the Victoria ground. And Stoke City, despite being only a smallish club, always seemed to prove difficult for Tottenham to beat.

So it was just Shaun, Pricey, Freemo, Hollins, Dave Ward and Cowboy who boarded the eight-fifteen from Worcester Shrub Hill station to Birmingham New Street. There they had to change to the Stoke-bound train. Enough time to raid an offie for supplies.

A couple of the lads had brought along cans and so these were shared out on the slow, stopping train to the second city.

As usual, the lads exchanged stories and news from the previous week. There had been a bit of a row on Paddington station, but nothing much. Freemo's wife, Julie, who often came along to games, had a bad cold and had stayed in bed. Smiffy was working and needed the overtime money. No one had seen Spence or Buzz. Just chit chat really.

Even though this was a slow train, the journey just wasn't long enough for a serious game of cards and so, once the small talk was over, the lads opened their papers as they drained their few cans. They always read newspapers from the back, working towards the front. Probably every avid football fan does the same. And most of them bored of the content once the sports pages ran out, then skipping forward to look at the tits on page three. Then possibly back to the problem page. Sometimes glancing at the TV pages to see which was to be the main game on Match of the Day that evening. One or two, occasionally, read the front page headlines too. But not often. Lots of football fans will recognise that reading pattern.

On arrival in Birmingham the first task was to find out about their onward connection options. The journey on to Stoke took about an hour and three quarters. It was still only just after nine and they wanted to arrive in time for a good drink.

New Street station was almost deserted at that early hour on a Saturday. Birmingham City were at home that day but it was still way too early to worry about blue noses fans being out and about for a home game.

Dave Goof disappeared off to find out the necessary connection information: time of departure, time of arrival, if the train had a buffet car. If he had enough time, he would probably find out the time of the return trains too.

Whilst he was away, Pricey casually asked a guy on a ticket barrier (amazingly, they had all bought tickets this week) if he happened to know the time of the next train to Stoke. As luck would have it he did. It would be leaving at 9:21 from platform three. He wasn't sure, though, if there would be a buffet car. Result! The lads burst into action. They had fourteen minutes to work in. They quickly passed through the barrier and out on to the station concourse, knowing that there was an off licence there which always seemed to be open.

And it was. An hour-and-three-quarters was a three to four can journey they estimated. Better safe than sorry and so they settled on four. They discovered that Carlsberg lager was on special offer – six cans for the price of four and a bit. So instead of buying six lots of four (they couldn't forget to get Dave a share), they opted for four lots of six. The lads tried to sort the money out on the spot, but the maths proved a little too complicated for their fuzzy heads. Besides, it was still early. In the end, Freemo paid for the lot and the lads agreed to work it all out on the train.

Six minutes to go! They surged back through the ticket barriers, only too be met by Dave Goof – looking smug and idly swinging a six pack of Carlsberg in a carrier bag. "They're on special offer lads". He grinned his toothy grin. "I didn't get you any as I couldn't carry them all". Bastard!

But just at this moment, Hollins and Freemo made it through the barrier, complete with twenty four bargain cans. Goof's face dropped – he hadn't managed to put one over on them after all. Bollocks. The lads smiled. The greedier amongst them could now have a fifth can. But it would fuck up the maths something terrible.

Dave quit on the smugness and tried serious. "Quick lads! 9:18 from platform two" he said urgently.

"Bollocks Dave! It's 9:21 and it leaves from platform fucking three! We've still got four minutes mate" retorted Pricey.

Goof's little revenge play to cause a panic hadn't worked either and he was inwardly annoyed. He managed a smile though and the group made their way on to the correct train with a whole minute to spare.

Before they had settled into their seats the train pulled out of the station on its journey northwards. The lads had walked through a surprisingly busy train, trying to find six seats together. With a table for cards.

As they neared the buffet car in the middle of their train they met some more of the Midlands Spurs – Clarkie from Leamington, Mick and Chris from Kidderminster, Aidy from Coventry. Sensible Keith and Steve (Stevesham) from Evesham. Bradley from Stroud. The usual culprits.

A game of cards soon broke out – first seven then the more serious three card brag. The groups swapped newspapers. Mick read the broadsheets and no one else wanted his. No tits. No problem page. Long words. A few tired jokes did another circuit. The occasional new one even got a laugh. So the journey passed fairly quickly, even though the train seemed to stop at even the most God-forsaken places (where no-one got on or off!). What WAS the point?

Eventually they arrived at Stoke-on-Trent's main station at ten past eleven. The lads knew it well enough. Turn right out of the main entrance, up the little hill for two hundred yards, across the busy road was a man's boozer – The Roebuck. They usually holed out there until the football specials arrived from London. There was quite often a bit of defending to do until reinforcements arrived, but that was fun. Repel all boarders! And once the specials arrived Spurs completely ruled the roost. Today there were two and there would also be plenty of Tottenham fans on service trains too – avoiding the gaze of the Police and their hungry looking dogs on the specials. You could add to that those who travelled by car and coach. Plus non-London based Spurs fans such as themselves. All in all a very handy mob for the annual running battle in the cemetery later.

But as the lads approached the Roebuck, they saw that it was all boarded up. Looked like it had been shut down for quite some time, too. What to do? They didn't want to walk too far towards town because of potential attacks and because they needed to rendezvous with the fans on their way up from London.

Freemo came up with a plan of sorts. Almost opposite the main station entrance was a posh hotel – The Victoria. He had been in there once, trying to impress some girl or other. The Victoria was four star and had thick carpets and Wedgwood Jasperware pieces in glass cases. The beer was fucking expensive, but it was beer all the same. And they served non-residents (who wouldn't be there long).

So the plan was that the thirteen thirsty lads split into groups of threes and fours. They would all hide their colours, polish their shoes on the back of their jeans and walk in at five minute intervals.

Clarkie, Hollins, Dave Goof and Freemo went first. Dave had a crimplene suit jacket and hush puppies (not trainers) and so probably – outwardly at least – was the most respectable. They breezed in confidently and turned right, walking straight through to the lounge bar Freemo had remembered.

Clarkie had the gift of the gab and so he ordered the lads four pints as the other three settled respectably into plush fireside armchairs. The white coated barman didn't bat an eyelid. Until, that is, Clarkie accidentally slammed the glasses down on the glass top of the Wedgwood display case. He couldn't disguise a worried grimace then, but Clarkie very quickly smoothed things over with a smilingly shamefaced apology.

Carefully transferring the drinks to a proper table, they studiously ignored Shaun, Pricey and Cowboy who, it seemed, had not been able to wait the full five minutes. They, too, were served with no problem and took their seats as the relay continued.

If the barman suspected anything, he was certainly too polite to say so and, after around fifteen minutes, his custom had swelled from an empty lounge area to eighteen to twenty nice enough lads; almost cultured.

Stevesham made the same glasses-on-cabinet faux pas, but nothing serious went wrong. Gradually the distinct little groups stopped ignoring each other as they relaxed and moved closer together. Others – Tottenham fans who they didn't know – came in too.

The barman must have been delighted with the morning's takings as forty to fifty thirsty blokes significantly boosted his commission. Colours began to show – the fire made it too hot to keep jackets on for any length of time. Still the barman didn't seem to have a problem. The seemed a good natured bunch. He did draw the line at the card game though – Pricey had produced a deck and the game was in full swing before the barman stepped in to stop it. "No gambling licence you see Sir" he politely explained. The lads understood.

The first football special arrived at around one o'clock. About a thousand chanting, bescarved Tottenham fans spilled out to be faced with a cordon of Policemen on horses. And snarling German Shepherd dogs on very long leashes.

Some of the lads in the hotel bar left and joined the Londoners as they made their way towards the ground. Around a hundred more Midlands and Northern Spurs joined them at the top of the road. A handy firm. As it was escorted to the ground little groups broke off and made their way to back street pubs which all seemed to smell of coal. Some were rounded up; others weren't.

The Worcester lads decided, despite the extortionate prices, to stay and wait for the second special, due in another forty minutes.

There was a little more space in the bar now, but it very soon began getting full up again. The forty minutes flew by – the lads were quite pissed and the special was due any minute. So they politely thanked the barman and headed back out onto the railway station.

The second special was full, too and a few service trains from London had also disgorged a few hundred more Tottenham boys.

The second mob of around fifteen hundred strutted and chanted their way through the strange city that is Stoke. It is a disjointed place made up of a number of small pottery towns: Stoke itself, Burslem, Hanley and a couple of others no-one can remember. It never seemed to have a centre like other places. And everywhere was fucking grimy.

The Stoke lads – from the Boothen end of the ground – were always a bit backward. This was 1980 and they still wore wide-legged trousers and black motoring gloves on one hand. Northern Soul boys. They weren't viewed as hard, but they were usually game.

Every year they attempted to attack football specials at the same point on the way to the ground. They weren't too bright it seemed and, as the lads passed the low cemetery wall on the left, they were never surprised when about two to three hundred widely-trousered youths stormed across the graveyard lobbing half bricks from leather gloved hands.

The next sequence in the annual dance was Old Bill trying to stop the Tottenham fans from retaliating by somehow getting their dogs to bark ferociously. Finally, they would be ignored. Tottenham would swarm over the wall into the cemetery and, using discarded Stoke ammo, would return fire. The Stoke numbers would dwindle to less than fifty as the two groups joined battle. And still further as the first, bravest, two were punched and ran away. Spurs never seemed bothered enough to finish the job off and chased the Stoke just far enough away to stop a second attack before the game. That would come on the way back. But the result was always similar: Lots of tired Stoke legs; two Stoke black eyes; four Spurs bitten arses. Not worth the bother really.

After the bit of sport, the lads did attempt a break away from the middle of the marching mob but were quickly rounded up by rabid looking dogs attached to pissed off Policemen. Fuck it!

They were, eventually, escorted all the way to the away end of the Victoria Ground; made to queue; searched for weapons and then virtually corralled into the fenced in area that was reserved for away fans.

The Victoria was a crappy little affair. Compact with a reasonable atmosphere and a fair view, but it had little else going for it. Smelly open air bogs. Fences everywhere. Inadequate refreshment facilities. But they DID serve beer underneath the terraces. And there was still nearly half an hour before kick off, so plenty of time for one. Or two.

At ten-to-three the lads drained their plastic glasses and fought their way out to a good vantage point on the packed Tottenham terraces. They liked to stand directly in front of the crush barriers and so, if there was a surge from the back, it stopped just behind them. They also liked the barrier to be close to a gangway. Easier to get out for a piss and a beer at half time. Eventually they found a spot they approved of – just as the teams came out onto the pitch.

The Tottenham end erupted into cheers, fluttering ticker tape and then songs. One by one the fans chanted the players songs and cheered wildly as that player responded with a quick wave of acknowledgement. The announcement of the Stoke team lead to eleven bouts of booing. And there was a loud cheer for each Spurs player announced. Game on.

The game wasn't exactly a pushover for Spurs that day. But it was quite entertaining and in the end lowly Stoke were beaten 3-2 by the mighty Spurs. The bar didn't re-open at half time though. The queues for the bogs meant that they nearly missed the start of the second half. And the fucking pies were cold.

Tottenham fans were kept in for ten minutes after the final whistle, much to their annoyance. After this they were marched back, either to the coach park or to the train station. Those in cars had one hell of a job persuading the Police that they weren't trying to pull a flanker – literally – on the home fans.

The expected second leg of the battle of the cemetery took place. Only two fans seemed to get bitten this time out of the couple of thousand who repelled the graveyard attack. And a few more Stoke were caught by the disgruntled away fans. Bit of a result then really.

On arrival back at the station Old Bill tried to force everyone onto the first special train. The lads had to show their train tickets to Worcester to stop themselves being packed off to London. The first and then soon after the second specials left. A couple of London bound service trains quickly followed. The police wanted the troublesome Londoners gone.

The lads couldn't get near a train to Birmingham yet. They explored the hotel opposite, but it was now firmly shut – at least to them. Too much trouble in the town during the day.

Finally, the thirteen lads who had arrived together (plus three or four other Spurs stragglers) found themselves on a bench on a draughty platform one, waiting for their train.

To their right were thirty or forty Stoke City fans, but the lads weren't worried. Stoke were wankers. But without them noticing, the Stoke numbers swelled to over fifty. Suddenly, they filled the platform and began to walk menacingly towards the Tottenham group.

"Don't run!" said someone urgently. But there was no need. Without exchanging a word, fifteen lads lined up in single file across the platform and walked forward to meet the threat. There was no way out anyhow as the Stoke had blocked off the entrance.

Seemingly unphased by being outnumbered more that three-to-one, the Tottenham group tried their best to look frightening. Snarling. Screaming. The Stoke firm, initially very confident due to their numbers, began to falter. These Spurs fuckers must be mental! Those at the front broke stride. Those at the back turned left through the station exit. No Police protection now boys. Lets get it on!

Seeing their rivals falter was the signal for Spurs to attack. They launched themselves the final fifteen feet at the Stoke and begun punching anything in sight.

That did it! The Stoke fans ran like rabbits, startled by their mad opponents. All except one, that is. The one Clarkie picked on. Stoke ran everywhere – even onto the railway lines – to escape the marauders. Except Clarkie's one. Now Clarkie was never scared of a

19

row, but even he would admit he was never the best scrapper. He and his opponent (they seemed of similar ability) stood toe-to-toe, exchanging occasional feints and body swerves as the rest of the Stoke fans were routed all around them. Laughing victoriously, the rest of the lads came back and finished off Clarkie's guy with a couple of deft swats to the ear. He ran.

"Fucking hell lads!" moaned Clarkie. "I had him there! Why did you have to interfere?".

"Well, from what we saw" answered one of the lads "neither of you had landed a punch for the last five minutes!".

Even Clarkie had to half agree as they all jumped back onto the train home. It had been a fucking good day.

Result : Stoke City 2 – 3 Tottenham Hotspur (Hughton, Archibald,

Taylor (pen))

Attendance : 18,614

Oh and by the way...

~

The football season had finished and next week was Cup Final week. At the final game of the season, Smiffy invited all the lads to watch it at his house. They all arranged to meet in Worcester's 'White Hart' at around one on Cup Final day.

Everyone turned up, loaded with a few cans to take back for the match. The lads drunk happily for an hour or so and then piled into Smiffy's car for the short trip to his home.

As they neared, Smiffy pulled the car up a few hundred yards short of his house. "I've got something to tell you lads" he said seriously. "Well hurry up – it's only ten minutes to kick-off" said an impatient Hollins.

"You know after the football last week?, Well I haven't actually been home since". Smiiffy was married (to Julie) and had a son. And he'd been off bonking all week.

"Fucking hell, Smiffy! Will she let us in?".

"No idea, actually" replied the embarrassed driver. "We haven't spoken about it".

"Well you'd better fucking try mate! Get your arse up there and see." said the unsympathetic lads.

So Smiffy drove the final few yards home, pulled the car up outside and gingerly approached the front door as the lads stayed put in the car.

First he rang the bell. Then he knocked. Then he shouted through the letterbox. Then he hammered on the door. Nothing. But Freemo had seen the upstairs curtains twitch.

He appeared at Smiffy's side. "Fuck off out of it Jim" he said as he took up position at the letterbox.

"Julie. It's me, Freemo. I know you're in there darling. Smiffy's just told us what happened. He's a right tosser. But he promised we could watch the Cup Final here. And it's nearly kick off. Please?".

The upstairs window suddenly opened and they heard a voice from behind the curtains. "Well, you can watch it Freemo. But that bastard's not coming in".

"Fine". shouted back Freemo. He gestured to the lads to come up the path and the door opened. "Er not you, Jim" Freemo said. "You've apparently still got some negotiating to do". The door shut behind the other lads and the domestic continued raging through the letterbox as the match was played out. She let him in before half time.

~

CHAPTER TWO

WE'RE ON OUR WAY TO WEMBLEY!
F.A. CUP SEMI-FINAL VS. WOLVES
(11/4/1981)

Freemo always fancied himself as a bit of an artist. Everyone seemed to agree that he made a fine piss artist, but real, proper art? Nah! For this game he had drawn (and made loads of copies of) a cockerel choking a wolf. That was BOUND to annoy the Wolves fans! Worcester, where the lads were based, is less than forty miles from Wolverhampton and so there were a fair number of Wolves fans in the city too. The ritual Friday evening Sainsbury's trip was accomplished safely. A couple of the lads would go with Smiffy and buy loads of beer and wine for the journey. It saved a lot of time the next day and stayed cold if it was left in the boot overnight). The lads had then toured round town on the Friday night, finalising plans for the next day and annoying any stray Wolves fans they happened to see. It was going to be a long day next day and so they didn't bother asking the landlord for their usual Friday night lock-in – they had to be up early. Sheffield was over 200 miles away and not all the lads had managed to get tickets - they needed to be there early to see what could be scored from the touts.

Smiffy sleepily went round the houses to pick up the lads one by one. This week it was him, Freemo, Hollins, Spence and Squeezy. Freemo jnr. had no money but the others decided to let him go along anyhow… on the understanding that he was barman (he had to open and pass cans round as required. Sometimes he would be allowed one himself). And that, if the car was too crowded, he'd have to travel in the boot. The lads sometimes did that – someone in the boot, not shut and held down by a shoelace so there was plenty of air. They had plenty of beer in there so it wasn't too bad. Saved hiring a bigger car.

And so the uncomfortably full Ford Cortina swung onto the M5 shortly after eight-thirty – six uncomfortable blokes, lots of beer and a few hundred crap cartoons crammed in as best as possible.

The lads bantered good humouredly as the motorway miles were eaten up. They were across to the M1 not long after ten and the traffic going north was now littered with football fans, scarves flying from car windows. Not just Spurs – the Wolves fans were travelling up by the same route and so the lads took great delight in holding up Freemo's cartoons every time they passed a Wolves car at a speed where the opposition would be able to see them. Smiffy never hung about. They might miss opening time! The pictures invoked a variety of hand signals from the Wolves car windows – some seemed to shake sauce

28

bottles. Others flexed their archery fingers – some even placed their over-sized arses against the windows. But the lads soon tired of baiting them and settled into happy banter and a few cold cans. Besides, it was fucking uncomfortable to keep moving the pictures with six in the car.

On this day the lads DID just miss opening time, thanks to heavier than expected traffic as they neared Sheffield. Smiffy drove straight to the ground and worked on a parking space within reasonable walking distance from the ground – he normally managed to squeeze them in somewhere and today was no different. Safely parked behind one of the tenement blocks which blight the area near Sheffield Wednesday's ground, the lads went in search of two spare tickets for Squeezy and Freemo jnr. And got a result almost straight away. Freemo jnr. scored one from a Spurs fan whose friend had let him down and not turned up at the station that morning. Squeezy paid only a little over the odds from a tout, but both tickets were Spurs end ones and genuine – the lads checked them against their own tickets before handing over their cash.

Freemo had managed to get hold of two tickets in the 'posh' stand on the side through a contact at work. The spare was allocated to Smiffy. Spence and Hollins got tickets through Tottenham.

So, all ticketed up, the lads set off in search of a few pre-match beers. The Police and many of the already assembled Spurs fans had told them that all the pubs in the area were closed for the day, but that didn't deter them. Fuck it – they'd find one, or if not they'd search out an off licence! But gradually they began to realise that ALL the pubs (and offies) really WERE closed. They walked miles, not really knowing where they were going. On passing the car for the third time, they decided to salvage a couple of cans from the boot. Things were desperate!

Soon the return journey supplies ran out. Long queues were building at the Tottenham fans end of the ground. Decision time. Reasoning that beer may be on sale inside the ground, the lads decided that they might as well go in and try. Freemo and Smiffy left the other lads jostling in the queue for the terraces behind one goal and strolled up to the turnstiles to the posh area. They were able to walk straight in, picking up their free programme as they went. Smiffy soon spotted the magic 'Bar' sign! Yahoo! And it wasn't just one of those lean-up-against-a-wall-drinking-warm-expensive-beer-from-a-plastic-glass bars. This one was like a pub – proper bar, proper glasses, northern prices. Even tables and chairs. Result! With an hour and a half to go until kick off, the two lads happily swigged lager as their minds turned to football. Spurs had struggled in the previous round versus lowly Exeter City. They remembered Warren Mitchell, dressed as Alf Garnett, geeing up the Tottenham fans at half time when the score was still nil-nil. Whilst Alf was West Ham, Warren Mitchell was a lifelong Spurs fan and season ticket holder. Anyhow an injury to their main striker and a couple of late goals saw Spurs scramble through. Wolves weren't classed as a big club and Tottenham were favourites to go through to the centenary Wembley F.A. Cup final. The lads decided – through a lager fuelled haze – that they were confident.

They climbed the stairs to the main stand and took their seats at about ten to three. Great seats on the halfway line. The bar was opening at half time too! As they looked round the ground, they saw that it was two-thirds full of Spurs. The whole of one end, all of the side they were on and just over half of the other side of the ground. Advantage Tottenham!

The game ebbed and flowed. The lads lost their voices. Hibbit fucking dived for an equalising penalty. After extra time, the game finished in a disappointing 2-2 draw. Bollocks! That meant a replay would be necessary. Wolves had cheated. Spurs hadn't played well, despite fanatical support booming from three sides of the ground. But they had easily done enough to have won. Double bollocks!

The dejected lads trudged back to the parked car, muttering as they went. The two sets of fans were strictly segregated and so there was no chance of a row to let off some steam. The boot was empty – no more beers. They faced a long, uncomfortable car journey and none of them was in the best of moods.

Freemo jnr. copped the brunt of it as he was banished to the boot to make things more comfortable for the paying passengers. Sighing, he dutifully removed a shoelace to use as a boot catch. The lads cleared out all the debris from the boot and in he climbed. Once they had

30

made sure he was OK, they crammed back into the car – it was still tight with five big lads in – and struck out for home.

Freemo and Smiffy sniggered quietly as they discovered that there was no beer on sale on the main terraces. The other lads had watched the game sober for probably the first time in a good many years.

The football traffic was very slow so when the car passed an open off licence, Smiffy pulled over and the lads replenished their supplies. They even passed a couple of tins to Freemo jnr. as he climbed back into the boot after stretching his legs (jnr. was 6'2" tall, despite his age).

They reached the outskirts of Sheffield still crawling, beer supplies running dangerously low again. Fucking hell!

At long last the car joined the queue for the motorway, made worse by the fact that this was the point where the two sets of fans converged on their journeys home. Revitalised by their cans, the lads dug out the tattered cartoons and began baiting Wolves fans again. More sauce bottles and more archers.

The traffic began to move a little quicker once they had joined the motorway – maybe twenty miles an hour now! Smiffy did his best and tried to keep positioning them in the fastest moving lane of traffic, but inevitably it was pot luck.

One particularly aggressive car load of Wolves boys kept overtaking – and then being overtaken by, the cartoon wielding lads. The two drivers began cutting each other up and the lads began getting seriously annoyed. Smiffy was ahead of them now and pulled away – only to be held up by stationary traffic around the next bend.

The Wolves lads were up for it, or at least their driver was. He pulled up right behind the lads. Horn blaring, lights flashing. Both drivers got out of their cars and strode towards each other like John Wayne in the middle lane of the M1. Showtime!

Inevitably it kicked off. Smiffy was doing OK until the Wolves driver pulled his jumper over Jim's head. Ever seen a windmill in motion?

31

That was Smiffy, punching the air furiously in an effort to whack his unseen opponent.

The three other Wolves boys got out of the car and so Freemo raced out, deftly kicked their driver up the arse and gave him a backhander. By this time, the other Worcester lads had got out of the car. Five Spurs and four Wolves stood face to face on the motorway. The other traffic had moved off and passing motorists were – to say the least – a little bemused by the scene.

The Wolves fans were weighing up their chances – not too sure now. And then the lads car boot opened. Freemo jnr. emerged, car jack in hand. Fair play to him. This was all too much for the Wolves firm who legged it back to the safety of their car, chased by the lads.

The Wolves fans made it first and clicked their four doors locked in a flash. Sanctuary!

Except for the poor driver that is. He was sitting smugly in the car, not realising that he had left his window open. Freemo caught him with a right hander and he smashed across the car into his passenger. Jnr. started wrecking the car, but older bruv. told him to cool it. They had won – and scared the opposition witless. No point in vandalism.

So the lads sauntered back to their car. They even allowed Jnr. back in the main car. There was much to discuss. And they needed a barman.

By the time the fracas was over, traffic had begun to move much more freely. The lads pulled off with a few final (and reciprocated) rude gestures and that was the last they saw of the Wolves fans, who must've kept a respectable distance behind until their two paths diverged.

After all the excitement, the rest of the journey home was uneventful. One more off licence stop and a couple of quickies in a pub just off the M5 and they were home with just enough time for a couple more in Worcester.

They couldn't plan the replay journey as all that was known was that it would be at the despised Highbury ground. "It'll cost me a fucking fortune in disinfectant after that game!" Freemo said gravely. Peter Cook may have got his famous quote from this.

Result : Wolverhampton Wanderers 2 – 2 Tottenham Hotspur (Archibald, Hoddle)

Attendance : 40,174

FOOTNOTE : Spurs won the replay 3-0 at Highbury (15/4/1981) in front of a crowd of 52,539. Garth Crooks scored two and Ricky Villa the other. Freemo bought disinfectant for decontamination purposes.

Oh and by the way…

~

Spence and Pauline decided to marry in her home town of Arbroath. The popular couple arranged a full sized coach to transport friends from Worcester. Freemo was already living in Yorkshire and so was making his own arrangements. Smiffy and Lesley didn't like coach travel and so decided to drive 'half way' up to Freemo's and cadge a lift from there. Freemo's company car was easily big enough for them all to travel in comfort.

The coach load and the carload of friends were all booked into adjacent small hotels and B&Bs and the was a pub conveniently close by. By chance, everyone arrived at about the same time on the morning of the wedding. The fifty travellers all checked in, showered, changed into wedding clothes…. and went to the pub to wait for the others.

The wedding was to be at 3 o'clock and so the friends drank happily for an hour and a half. They had seen the church at the end of the road and guessed it was only two minutes away. They could easily leave at ten to three and get there politely early.

The lads got more into their drinking. The girls began to fret as time passed. To gain another five minutes, all the lads secretly put their watches back ten minutes. When the girls disagreed with the time, all the other lads showed their watches and so the girls believed them.

At just before ten to three by the lads watches, they sank their pints and hurried on to the church at the end of the road. No one was there. They knocked and asked. Wrong fucking church! They were given directions to the correct church – five minutes away.

And that's how fifty friends, in various states of fitness – charged past the arriving bride and into the music filled church. Ten minutes or more late. Thank goodness for the bride's customary late arrival.

The wedding was a large one and everything went according to plan. At the reception, the English friends had been seated together on two long trestle tables. The rest of the room was filled with Scots. It was all very friendly until the apparently Scottish tradition of filling-in-the-gap-between-afternoon-and-evening-parties-by-doing-your-party-piece began.

The sweaties all got up and, firmly inserting a finger in one ear, began singing songs of Bannockburn and the like. The English party took offence, but to their credit decided against ruining the occasion with a punch up. So they just walked out and found a pub to wait in until the evening party started. Flicking the Vs as they went.

~

CHAPTER THREE

MANCHESTER CITY
THE F.A. CUP FINALS
(9 & 14/5/1981)

Tottenham had made it to Wembley again! Was there REALLY something in this 'lucky for Spurs when the year ends in one' stuff after all??

Their opponents were to be Manchester City. Well enough supported; useful enough, but Tottenham's legions of fans expected to beat them fairly comfortably.

There was, of course, the usual scramble for tickets. Habitually Spurs gave out vouchers at the less attractive home fixtures a few weeks before the May final. They then held a ballot for those remaining tickets after players, staff and season ticket holders had claimed theirs. Each club was usually allocated around 35,000 tickets for Wembley F.A. Cup finals, with any remaining going to local F.A.s throughout the U.K. These organisations usually allocated a couple each to all their affiliated clubs, whose players fought over them. And that's how Hollins managed to get hold of three, with the help of a little bribery and blackmail. He blagged another for Lloydy – a local referee who he got on well with.

Freemo had recently joined Grattan, the catalogue company, from Kays. He had been one of a management team of twenty who moved from one company to the other. All of his colleagues knew of his fanatical support for Spurs, including Swaino (the Financial Director) and David Jones (the M.D.). David had excellent contacts. Freemo had approached Swaino to make it known he was desperate for tickets. Swaino said that he couldn't promise anything but that he would mention it.

And - joy of joys – Freemo turned up for work one day to find tickets for two great seats on his desk, still a couple of weeks before the game. Overjoyed, Freemo asked what he owed. "You couldn't afford it Malc" answered Swaino. "Even David had to go out and buy those on the black market. And believe me they were NOT cheap. He said to enjoy the game, on him".

Freemo was overwhelmed. Such efforts on his behalf from someone who was so busy and so important bought a lot of loyalty and extra effort. He worked hard and, in return, was well rewarded, but this was something very special to him. Something he would never forget.

40

The other lads took their chances in the ballot and/or used their contacts to get hold of tickets. One or two had to pay over the odds on the black market. But, remarkably, everyone managed to turn up trumps in the end – even those lads who didn't go to games so regularly.

Some wanted to travel down by car. Some wanted to organise a coach. The lads decided on their usual mode of transport and so Smiffy hired a car. One of those fucking horrible, no-headroom-in-the-back Ford Capris. But new and reliable. With a bit of a boot to carry the beers.

The evening before the final Smiffy picked up first the car, then the lads for the by now ritual Sainsbury's trip. The car boot was filled with cans of lager (around eight each), bottles of wine (around one each) and a bottle of something unusual (one for the whole car). This week it was Whisky Mac – a mixture of cheap whisky and ginger wine. The lads custom was, at some stage of the journey, to open the 'unusual' or guest bottle and pass it round the car – everyone taking swigs in turn – until the bottle was completely drained. No breaks. No stopping. It usually took five to ten minutes. The lads usually conducted this ritual towards the end of the journey down to the match, as it involved the driver too. They didn't want Smiffy too pissed too early. And he'd have time to recover before it was time for him to drive home.

So their boot was filled with supplies and then the lads had a few beers in town to excitedly discuss the next day's big game. Not too many though – they needed to get up early; arrive early; get in the pub early; get in the stadium (fairly) early to experience the atmosphere – it was always great at Wembley.

Because Tottenham are a London club, their fans get hold of more tickets when their opponents are out-of-towners. The lads reckoned Spurs might have as many as ten thousand more fans inside the stadium than Manchester City.

They discussed the team THEY would pick (Ricky Villa was blowing hot and cold – should he start?); what formation they would play (almost unanimously 4-4-2); what kit they would wear (Man City played in pale blue shirts and white shorts. Were the kits too similar for T.V.?); who should be subs (some for if Spurs went a goal down. Some for closing the game out if they went one up); where to park (the general consensus was that nobody but Smiffy could give a flying fuck).

One by one the lads headed for home. None of them before nine-thirty, but none of them much after ten. Scarves to dig out. Boots to polish. But, most importantly, a good night's sleep to get.

All too soon, Smiffy was sounding the horn outside their houses. Smiffy was the only one of them who was half human much before ten. The others usually struggled, but not today.

Today was the reason that they gave their money, hearts and souls (and legs, feet and heads, hopefully) for the common cause. Their cockerel clad chests would swell with pride as hoards of white and navy wearing fans greeted their team as they entered the arena. A tear would reach their eyes as the songs rolled down from the packed terraces, drowning out the efforts of their northern opposition. And Tottenham would be giving something back to their legions of loyal fans. Surely.

The Capri made good time, despite the unusually large number of piss-stops. As they hit the outskirts of London, Spence was well ahead in the farting competition, after recovering from dodgy guts earlier in the week. Or maybe you should consider it a relapse, depending on your perspective. Anyhow, he stunk like a skunk with sonic accompaniment which any session percussionist would be proud of. Thought he'd ripped his trousers at one stage. The other lads could only applaud.

Smiffy decided the car park issue for them and pulled into the large NCP that the whole world seemed to use at cup finals and England games. Very easy to get into. A bastard to escape from. It could easily take an hour, even if you allowed time for the traffic to subside. Anyhow, that's what he wanted to do and so that's where they parked up, despite the lads having now developed opinions on the matter.

Habitually the lads made for 'The Torch' whenever they went to Wembley. It was a big pub. There wasn't usually much trouble and – if you happened to be a bit skint – you could buy cans from the cheap offie over the road and drink them in the car park.

It was a good idea to get there as early as possible and take up a good position. Either near the bar doors (for an easier fight to get drinks) or near the uphill entrance to the car park (for trips to the offie and/or the burger stand plus a place to sit on the wall). The Torch was the place that the lads had arranged to meet everyone else from Worcester who had travelled down by different means.

And so they, opting for the car park entrance option, took up position and began blowing the froth off a few cans. Carrier bags from the offie at their feet.

Generally, all the Worcester boys made the rendezvous. And their were friends from all over the U.K. who joined their party. The Micks from Warrington, Sensible Keith and Stevesham, Phil, Richie and the Uxbridge crew, Joe and the Oxford boys, John and the Swindon contingent, the Wolverhampton Spurs – everyone turned out.

The Police hadn't deemed it necessary to segregate the pubs for this fixture and the Torch's car park was brimming over with football fans. This particular pub happened to be 70% plus Tottenham, but there was no hint of trouble from either set of supporters.

Everyone, it seemed, had made an effort to show their loyalty. White doctor's coats. Face paint. Stupid hats. Flags and banners. Spurs shirts. Scarves. Fair play.

The volume increased as the litter bins began to overflow with empty cans and bottles. Time passed quickly and soon – all too soon – it was time to leave for the traditional walk up Wembley Way to the stadium. They all wanted to be in position for that spine tingling moment when your team emerges from the tunnel. It's a moment football fans never forget. Unmissable.

So for once the lads took up their places on the huge terraces and waited. And sung.

And then came that wonderful moment. The teams appeared at the head of Wembley's tunnel. Pandemonium! All parts of the ground erupted at the same moment. Tottenham fans resurrected their Argentinian habit of throwing torn paper in the air for Ricky Villa and Ossie Ardiles. The lads had been furiously tearing up newspapers and stuffing the bits in carrier bags for just this moment.

It's a moment that can't be properly described to non-football fans. Armchair Manks or nouveau Chelsea fans just wouldn't appreciate the depth of it. They'd just pretend they did, like always.

It is a moment when your chest swells up with pride for your team; for your thousands of fellow supporters. You and they have made huge sacrifices and, for one moment at least, it seems like you have been paid back. With interest. That you DO count. It is, quite simply, a goose-bump, hair-standing-up-on-the-back-of-your-neck moment which only real supporters can share. And it was NOW!!

The noise was deafening. The paper fluttering on the breeze blocked out the sky. The Manchester City fans must have felt the same way – they loved their team too.

Emotions only just in check, the one hundredth F.A. Cup Final kicked off.

The match proved to be not as an exciting encounter as the experts had expected, although it did have its moments.....

Tottenham did most of the early attacking but still fell behind on the half hour as Hutchison dived full length to head home spectacularly. Despite all Spurs' efforts the lads feared the worst – they couldn't seem to put away any of their chances.

But in the eightieth minute Tottenham won a free kick outside the box. Ardiles shifted the ball to Perryman. Perryman teed it up and Hoddle, running in, bent the ball round the Manchester wall. Corrigan looked to have it covered but that man Hutchison, seeing the danger, dashed across goal. The ball struck him on the shoulder and deflected wickedly into the opposite corner. Hutchison, a 33 year old who was a £47,000 mid-season signing from Coventry, was distraught. Corrigan tried to console him whilst the lads – and around 60% of the stadium – went delirious! You could feel the tension evaporate. "Glory, Glory Hallelujah" echoed around the arena.

The draw was played out after extra time. Both sides had had chances to win, most memorably when City's Mackenzie rounded the keeper, beat Perryman to the ball... and contrived to hit the post from two yards out with the goal completely at his mercy. But neither side did and so, for only the tenth time in the F.A. Cup's rich history, the match was drawn.

The lads walked back to their car with mixed feelings. They were, of course, relieved at getting another chance, but were also worried on a number of counts. How would the replay go? Ricky Villa had been shit again and had been hauled off in the 68th minute (for Gary Brooke). Would they be able to get tickets for the replay? And when, exactly, would these tickets go on sale? Would they be able to get time off work for it? Most important, could they fucking win it!?

In the build up to the final, the bookies had made Tottenham warm favourites to lift the cup. There was a load of hype and media coverage of Ossie Ardiles winning 'the cup for Tottingham'. The lads had not even considered anything but yet another piece of silverware for Spurs. And so this was all a bit of a shock to the system.

They asked around and discovered that replay tickets were going on sale at ten a.m. the next morning, from Wembley Stadium only. In one way that was a result. Not as many Manks would be able to get there and buy tickets. On the other, lots more Londoners would be able to turn out, including those who were unable to get tickets for the original game. The replay tickets were to be sold on a first come, first served basis.

The lads debated staying over and sleeping in the car, but eventually decided on going back to Worcester for the night, getting up at six the next morning and coming back down. And so they set of for home. Once the car park had cleared, of course. And it took the best part of an hour and a half. Smiffy silently endured the 'told you so' digs as the lads disgruntledly bickered.

They arrived back in Worcester, despite only one short pub stop, too late for a nightcap. Smiffy dropped the lads all off somewhere near home. They had already discussed who was going back down the next day – not everyone could make it. Those who WERE going – Smiffy, Hollins, Spence and Freemo – arranged their early Sunday pick ups and turned it in the hope of half a good night's sleep. The four had promised to try to pick up any spares they could for those lads who couldn't go back to queue.

The next morning the four, via cashpoint stops, set back out for Wembley. For once beerless. For once not caring.

Two of them slept most of the way down. Freemo managed to stay awake and keep Smiffy company as he drove – he would be tired too. An because of this, Freemo won the farting contest with just one weak effort. The two discussed how long they might have to queue for. With any luck, getting to Wembley before nine o'clock would mean a short queue and so a quick getaway might be possible. They MAY even be able to get back to Worcester, lie about the length of time spent queuing and have a good few beers at lunchtime.

In any event the plan unravelled dramatically as they arrived at Wembley's huge car park. It was only a little after eight thirty and the queues were already snaking on for hundreds of yards. Fuck it!

As quickly as they could the four joined what seemed the shortest queue and began reading the Sunday tabloids they had managed to pick up on the way. Plenty of reports and pictures from the previous days final. It all seemed so long ago already! Someone wandered off and found coffees. It was a shame that the usual thriving Sunday market wasn't being held – that way they could have got full breakfasts whilst they waited.

As often happens, the long queues started shuffling forwards well before ten. The ticket sellers had looked at the queues and just decided to open up early. By quarter past ten, the lads were half way to the window and at quarter to eleven they had their precious tickets in their hands! But they had only been allowed to buy one each, so lots of their mates would be short.

46

After a quick discussion, the lads sighed and rejoined the back of the queue, intent on getting another four. As luck would have it, they didn't need to. Others had had the foresight to bully little brothers, sisters and their friends to queue with them and so were able to pick up plenty of spares. They approached the queue, asking only ten quid above face value. Faced with that or a two hour plus wait in the lengthening queue, the lads paid up and set off back to Worcester. Eight F.A. Cup final tickets safely in their wallets.

The carload arrived back on the outskirts of their city at not long after one o'clock and so, without the need for any discussion, Smiffy swung left into a convenient pub car park.

As the lads drank, they worked on who would get the spare tickets and drew up a prioritised list. The replay was being held on the following Thursday evening and people would need at least the Thursday afternoon off. Ideally they would take all day Thursday and Friday off. Thursday to travel at leisure. Friday to recover. But not everyone managed it, and so it wasn't until after one p.m. that the hire car set off again on the by now familiar trek.

The four spare tickets had gone to grateful mates, but they had had to make their own travel arrangements. For the same price the lads paid, of course. You didn't make money out of your own,

Tickets for the replay had completely sold out in just a few hours – it didn't help that the stadium capacity had to be reduced slightly for evening kick offs (apparently for safety reasons).

By four o'clock the lads had taken up almost exactly the same positions on the wall of 'The Torch' that they had assumed just five days earlier. They had visited the same off licence and drank the same lager, stored in the same carrier bags. In any other circumstances it might have been boring. But not on Cup final day!

Today the majority in favour of Tottenham in the pub was even bigger – it was almost exclusively full of Spurs fans, with just the occasional token Mank. All nice and friendly though.

The walk up Wembley Way – some insist on calling it by its proper name of Olympic Way, but it had always been Wembley Way to the lads – was very different too. As was usual on big Wembley final days, on Saturday each teams fans had walked the walk on opposite sides of the long road, waving flags and singing their respective songs. Today there was Tottenham everywhere. And because they outnumbered the northern fans by so much, the atmosphere was somehow more subdued. No one to out-sing.

Not until the lads reached the top of the road did they first realise that their tickets were in the Manchester City end. No wonder their queue had been the shortest! But having seen the large numbers of Spurs fans also queuing outside the same end they weren't too concerned.

As they fought their way on to the crowded terraces – there were still well over 90,000 people in the ground, despite the reduced capacity – they relaxed even more.

Apart from the end they were in, the entire stadium was full of Spurs fans. And their end was about one third Spurs too. A magnificent turn out – probably 70-75,000. The poor Citeh fans hadn't been able to get tickets or travel in big numbers.

Once more the stadium erupted as the teams came out. It seemed the roof must lift off! There was the odd minor scuffle at the Manchester end as the northerners seemed to suddenly realise just how many Tottenham fans were congregated in the middle and front of their terraces. But nothing serious.

This time the game lived up to expectation! Spurs started brightly and after just eight minutes took the lead. Steve Archibald's shot was only parried by the keeper. Ricky Villa – substituted and despairing only five days earlier – was first to react and followed up to poke home. Delirium!

But, as if to prove the old adage that you are at your most vulnerable when you've just scored, Tottenham conceded within just three minutes! City's Mackenzie scored with a spectacular volley to make the game all square again.

Half time arrived and, whilst both sides had had their chances, the score remained 1-1.

It didn't stay that way for long after the resumption. Within four minutes of the re-start the northerners had taken the lead. Paul Miller fouled Bennett in the area and referee Keith Hackett had no hesitation in pointing to the spot for only the fifth ever penalty in a Wembley final. Reeves put it away easily. 1-2. Bollocks. Here we go again.

Trouble broke out at the City end. Gloating City fans had gone a bit too far with their celebrations and were taking liberties. Some of the Spurs contingent turned on them and went toe-to-toe. But it didn't last long. Police and Stewards quickly calmed things down. And the City fans knew that they would have to get home safely after the game.

Tottenham pressed forward in an attempt to get the equaliser, having much of the possession. After seventy minutes, the ball broke to Garth Crooks. He poked home a scrappy goal to level the scores. Yahoo! Come on you Spurs!

Spurs now threw everything at City to try to force the winner as legs tired on the big pitch. Saturday's extra time was taking its toll. Things culminated in one of Wembley's greatest ever moments in the seventy sixth minute…

That man Villa collected the ball wide on the left and set off on an amazing dribble, bamboozling the entire City defence. The crowd held their breath. Corrigan tried to make himself big and stand up for as long as possible, but Villa coolly delayed his shot by half a second, despite City defenders scrambling to get back to him. And when Corrigan committed, Ricky Villa slipped his shot into the net and wheeled away in triumph. The noise was truly deafening. Some of the Manchester fans began to leave – a few feared a repeat of the violence, with the Spurs fans in their end reinforced by those in the rest of the stadium. More just believed that they were fated to lose. City should have won the first game, but didn't. They had fought back to lead from one down tonight, but STILL they were losing again with only fourteen minutes to go. And when they looked round the ground, all they could see were jubilant Tottenham fans everywhere. Singing, laughing, jumping wildly up and down. Rocking the very foundations of the old stadium.

Still Spurs attacked as the clock ticked down, but there was a heart-stopping moment close to the final whistle when City fired just wide of the right hand post.

Finally, after what seemed like several days, Hackett blew for full time. Spurs had won the cup!!

The runners up were sportingly clapped by the whole ground as they collected their losers medals and waved half-heartedly at the fast emptying Manchester end. City had put up on hell of a fight.

And then came that glorious moment. A beaming Steve Perryman thrust the glittering trophy skywards and the ground exploded for one last time. Grown men, including Freemo, had tears in their eyes. The team bounced up and down and sprayed champagne for the obligatory photograph and then set out on their lap of honour. The huge electronic scoreboard congratulated "Tottenham Hotspur – F.A. Cup Winners 1981" as the players, substitutes and management team were given a riotous standing ovation from all sections of the ground. As they reached each area, the crowd rose. It was like a slow motion Mexican wave. Of Tsunami proportions. Truly an unforgettable night.

No-one wanted to leave Wembley. Players included it seemed. But eventually they disappeared down the tunnel and the stadium finally began to empty.

So the lads walked happily back to the car park and began the hour plus wait for the traffic to begin moving. They had so much to talk about. They were so excited that they all talked at once. After fifteen minutes or so, Hollins and Freemo went off and found an off licence and picked up shed loads of beer for the journey home. Too late for the pubs now.

Eventually the stop-start traffic began to flow more freely and the lads struggled out on to the North Circular Road. By the time they reached Hangar Lane, the traffic was moving well on the Western Avenue and the journey home began in earnest.

It was well into the early hours of Friday as Smiffy dropped the lads off at their front doors. The most fabulous of days was over.

F.A. Cup Final – 9/5/1981

Result : Manchester City 1 – 1 Tottenham Hotspur (Hutchison, o.g.)
Attendance : 100,000

F.A. Cup Final Replay – 14/5/1981

Result : Manchester City 2 - 3 Tottenham Hotspur (Villa (2), Crooks)
Attendance : 96,000

Oh and by the way...

~

One week after a match on the South Coast, a bored and pissed Freemo and Spence decided not to go straight home.

They had discovered that Spurs were playing a friendly in Jersey on the Monday night and – as they had enough money with them, they made their way down to Poole for the Channel Island ferry, bought their tickets on the next departure and set out for the match.

They didn't book cabins and so spent most of the seven hour sailing drinking, sometimes playing the fruit machine.

It was winter and was bitterly cold on arrival in St Helier on the Sunday... and the place seemed to have closed down for winter. Apart from the big (expensive) hotels all other accommodation providers had apparently closed their doors until trade picked up again in Spring.

Dilemna! A plan was required. It involved first drinking several pints of Mary Ann at the unbelievably cheap price of 17p a pint. Stage two was to bang on the doors of cheap B&Bs and throw themselves on the mercy of whoever answered the door.

The first part of the plan went well, but the second wasn't so good. They tried numerous guest houses, but it seemed all were boarded up and deserted.

Finally, Spence managed to get a grumpy landlady to come to the door and explained their plight. And eventually, on hearing they only needed one night, she relented and let them a room so long as they agreed not to have breakfast.

The landlady said to come back in a couple of hours when she had aired the room and so the two went back to the warmth of the pub round the corner.

They returned as agreed and were shown to the dampest, coldest fucking room they had ever seen! The candlewick bedspreads steamed as the paraffin heater in the middle of the room tried its best with the damp. But at least it was a cheap bed.

Freemo and Spence spent most of Monday in Fort Regent drinking and playing snooker, with Spence cheating at every opportunity.

They made their way up to the football ground early and found the Tottenham team doing some light training. There were about fifty other Spurs fans there too and the players jogged over to shake hands and say hello. The lads were delighted.

The football ground was just one of those provincial pitches with a scaffolding pole perimeter. Not fenced off and free to get in. Someone was selling beers from a trestle table so the lads sat on the cold grass and watched the game.

No one took it too seriously, the players included. Tottenham won at a canter.

The ferry crossing home was very rough. Spence and Freemo started the same game of chess seven times. Seven times Spence resigned as he ran off – a victim of sea-sickness. He wasn't the only one. The ship's loo floor was totally covered in vomit as passengers queued to get in it.

Both Freemo and Spence were bollocked on two fronts – both for missing a day off work and also by their partners. They hadn't thought to mention that they were going away for a couple of days.

~

Result : Jersey Select XI 0 – 5 Tottenham Hotspur XI (Ardiles,
Archibald(3),
Brooke)

Attendance : Unknown (but under 1,000)

CHAPTER FOUR

THE TOTTENHAM HOTSPUR LAST SATURDAY HOME GAME BEFORE CHRISTMAS CLUB (MOTTO 'AD MORTUM')
(1981-Today)

The long title of this chapter will seem nonsensical to almost all readers, but please indulge me. I have used this short chapter to explain about this lads club which will be referred to throughout the lads series of books. It was founded in 1981 and is still going strong today.....

Freemo had been offered a job by colleagues at Kays who had moved to a rival catalogue company – Grattan. But it involved moving. To the North. Worse still, Yorkshire.

It proved a difficult decision – more money, company car, own office, a 10% starting bonus. But he had friends and family in Worcester. Lots of friends. His sister, Jan, had had her daughter Claire. She'd been in a bit of personal trouble and so Freemo and Julie let her stay with them to get her back on her feet. Claire was almost one now and Jan had settled down, so that bit was easier than it might have been.

Freemo talked to his friends. Almost all of them advised him to go and take the opportunity whilst it was there. He loved them for that.

And so, eventually, Freemo decided to make the move. He resigned from work and was immediately put on a months gardening leave. He spent most of that time with his brother Nigel, taking him to race meetings. Playing darts. Just spending some time together whilst they could. This was a time Freemo would remember gratefully twenty years later.

Of course, the burning question for the lads was how he was going to get to Spurs games. Not if, but how. Well, Freemo wouldn't be working Saturdays and there was a fast train from Leeds or Wakefield so he could definitely be there. Night matches would be difficult though. No car to book a seat in. No trains late enough. That would be a huge sacrifice.

As the move drew nearer, Freemo got more used to the idea and more comfortable with it. His sister got a great flat for her and Claire. Friends helped her do it up nicely. That made things easier. Things were good with bruv. Both insisted they would be up in Yorkshire as often as they could. And Freemo would be back in Worcester at least once a month.

The Thursday Night Married Men's Club arranged a little do at the Barbourne pub – a few sarnies and a few extra rounds of beer. Freemo was presented with a set of the pub's Banks's dominoes and a tray by the landlord. He was touched.

Before the off, Smiffy went out for a few quiet beers with Freemo and it was his idea which brought about The Tottenham Hotspur Last Saturday Home Game Before Christmas Club. Jimmy and Freemo decided to make a vow to have a good drink up together, at least once a year. They reckoned around Christmas would be a good time. And why not organise it to fit in with a Spurs game? They could watch a match too that way. But it would have to be a home game. It needed to be a Saturday game too as sore heads for Monday's work were never a good idea. And the kick off had to be at 3 o'clock to allow enough time for pre-match drinks and also to enable the lads to catch a train home the same night. And that has been the basis of the club from that day to this.

When the club was founded in 1981, there were just the two members and two rules: each member had to drink four cans of beer (or cider) on the train journey down. They also had to pin the four ring pulls to their lapel and wear them as a membership badge.

Meetings were set for 12 noon in the buffet bar on platform one (or was it eight?) of Kings Cross station. Freemo's train arrived there and it was also en route for Smiffy. At the first meeting in 1981, Tottenham beat Newcastle 3-1 and things just went on from there.

Further rules and club fines quickly developed. The word 'Duvodor' entered their vocabulary – a round of these double vodkas and orange juices had become the standard fine for any infringement of the rules.

Competitions were introduced. The members annually throw a penny from the platform of Seven Sisters tube. Level with the fourth roof support from the far end of the northbound platform. If they can land it so it stays on one of the rails, they win free drinks all day. As at 2008, no one has ever managed it.

The rules evolved to allow more members. Smiffy and Freemo were (are) full founder members and the only ones able to vote through changes to their rules. Hollins became the third full member with no voting rights). Smiffy became club treasurer. Richie Rich, Paul and Phill Holland, Crowbar, Ian Francis and Pete Buzz all came and went over the years. Membership was up to seven at one point.

A five pound bet (nowadays ten pounds) came into force, where each member makes a bet of their choice and donates all proceeds to the drinks kitty. It is the Treasurer's job to retain anything left over at the end of the day to kick off the next year's revelries.

Over the years there have been just too many stories to be able to tell them all her, but the most memorable include :-

Crowbar's expulsion due to falling asleep during the game two years in succession.

Hollins being thrown off the train home for accidentally pissing on the driver (he had been asleep and woke suddenly, desperate for the toilet. So desperate that he decided he would just have to throw open the door next to him and piss in the corridor. He threw the door open and began to relieve himself. Only then did he realise that he was in the driver's cab! The Police were waiting for him at the next station).

Jacko's arrest for abusing Derby County fans on Kings Cross station. (the Lads missed their trains home in an attempt to free him from custody, but, by the time they had tracked down the Police station where he was being held (just off the Marylebone Road for the record), Jacko had been cautioned and let go. He was already back in

Birmingham, trying to persuade his very Christian wife to come and pick him up. Being very economical with the truth).

Smiffy being presented with a travel alarm with a specially marked face after being consistently late for meetings. And losing it within two years.

The lads being caught with a hip flask of brandy in the front row of the East Stand lower. The steward emptied the contents onto the running track.

Sharing a joke or two with Statto, the TV football statistician, on the train from Seven Sisters to White Hart Lane.

Ignoring Hollins missus, Bid, the year he decided to bring her along. Women were against the rules.

Only one meeting has been missed in nearly thirty years. That was because Hollins had become very ill – he was officially recognised as an alcoholic at that stage. Smiffy and Freemo disbanded the club for a year, but secretly founded it again after that, reverting to the two of them being the only members. It was better for 'Ol that way. And every year, they raise a glass to him.

And that is how TTHLSHGBCC runs today. Nowadays, due to geography, they meet at Paddington station, not Kings Cross. You might see them there, bang on twelve, lapel badges proudly displayed at one of Spurs last Saturday home games around Christmastime. If you do, they drink Duvodors. Cheers.

FOOTNOTE : This chapter was written in November 2008 and, at the time of writing, Spurs had maintained a remarkably good record in these Christmas fixture. The only time they had lost was 0-2 to Liverpool, and then they could point the finger of blame at Steve Hodge who was sent off early in the game.

Another remarkable statistic that Smiffy managed to dredge up was that, in the five most recent years, Tottenham had won all the games and the team they beat went on to be relegated (Wolves 5-2, Southampton 5-1, Sunderland 3-2, Charlton 5-1 and Reading 6-4 (and yes, I KNOW it was just after Christmas, but a little flexibility was needed in 2007 due to the amount of Sunday games). It continues to amaze the author how the fuck ANYONE can remember ANYTHING after one of these meetings. Respect, Smiffy.

FOOTNOTE TO FOOTNOTE: (added in December 2008). Bollocks! We lost 0-1 to Everton this year. Me and my big mouth!

Shaun (sheepskin coat, walking away from camera), Freemo (pointing), Dave Goof and Cowboy outside the old entrance to the West Stand in the 1970s.

Every knew Bobby from Slough. Jovial bloke. Long straggly hair. Blue, nylon Starsky and Hutch style cardigan. Always pissed. Catchphrase "Faaack orrrfff!". THAT Bobby.

Well, Bobby had travelled with Tottenham to a European away game. After a days drinking with the Wolverhampton lads in German bars, Bobby was 'a little worse for wear'.

Two hours before the game he returned from the loo with a hand over his mouth. After much quizzing, he moved it to reveal a huge gap where his teeth used to be.

"What's happened Bob?", asked a laughing Graham.

"Threw up. Only lost me teeth down the faaackin bogs, haven't I?" came the spluttered response. The unsympathetic Midlanders fell about laughing, of course.

"Faaack orrrfff!".

So they did – it was getting on, with only an hour to kick off. The embarrassed Bobby was asked if he'd go with them, but turned it down, opting to stay for more drinks.

It was shortly after that the large clock on the pub wall stopped. Showing 58 minutes until the kick off. Bobby drank steadily, occasionally glancing at the clock to ensure he had time for another.

Finally, after two more hours, he had drunk enough and set off for the match. Approaching the stadium. He bumped into Graham, Pete, Popeye and the other Woverhampton lads walking back in the other direction. "Where you off to lads?" slurred Bobby. "The game has nearly fackin started!".

"Started??? It's just finished mate. Honest".

"Faaaack orrrfff!"

~

CHAPTER FIVE

ANDERLECT AWAY
U.E.F.A. CUP FINAL FIRST LEG
(4/5/1984)

Freemo and Julie – the blonde one, aka Julie One – travelled down from Yorkshire to the Midlands two days before the game. They had reserved spaces on Bradley's coach to the game and so it was that they arrived in Stroud – a sleepy town in Gloucestershire – late that evening.

It had been arranged that the coach would first pick up in Worcester (Shaun, the Wolverhampton and the Kidderminster lads) at 4:15 the next morning, picking up the Stroud contingent at 5. Because of this, the couple were offered a bed for the night by Bradley and his long-suffering wife Helen.

Not that night meant much to Mr. Bradley! The foursome went out on a mini pub crawl around town – lots of pubs but Freemo could only remember the Pelican. Oh, and a supermarket trolley came into it somewhere. Maybe.

So the 'night's accommodation' turned out to be a two-and-a-half-hour disturbed kip. In armchairs. The pregnant Helen wasn't coming with them on the trip, but she was still up at four, making sure that everyone else was awake; organising turns in the shower; making sure Bradley had packed a spare pair of underpants; rustling up a few rounds of under-cooked toast so the crunching noise didn't make the hangovers worse. A bloody good girl.

By five o'clock, Bradley, Julie and Freemo had staggered their half-asleep, half pissed, wholly grumpy way to the rendezvous point. It was early May and so at least it wasn't freezing cold. It wasn't pissing down either. The omens were good as the coach drew in to meet them. The sun was still an hour or two from showing its face.

Heads throbbing horribly, they clambered unsteadily up the few steps and onto the bus. Attempting smiles at the blurred faces towards the back of the fifty-two seater, Bradley settled into the seat next to the driver. The Freemos made it five rows further back before collapsing onto two seats in that row. Julie took the window and Freemo the aisle.

The bus now had ten or fifteen passengers on board – the Wolvo brothers Graham and Pete plus Popeye. From Kidderminster there were Micky G and Chris. There was Shaun and a few other lads from

Worcester. Just after 5 a.m. it pulled out of the lay-by, bound for the first of two pick ups in London.

As Freemo settled back into his seat, intent on a couple of hours sleep, a loud "shooooosh!" sounded in his left ear. Opening his eyes, a can of Banks's bitter had appeared – as if by magic – from the seat behind.

"Morning Freemo mate", chuckled the ever jovial Tommy Hall. "I saved you some breakfast!"

Freemo groaned, shut his eyes and turned away. "Fuck off Tommy!" he said with surprising venom. "I feel ill, now just fuck off!" he warned.

Tommy harrumphed his indignant way to the back of the bus where the others were, muttering loudly that Freemo was a "miserable bastard". But Tommy was never on to stay depressed for long – at least outwardly. Soon he was back in the seat behind Freemo, acoustic guitar in hand. Now, Chas and Dave were only ever acceptable because they were genuine Spurs fans, but Tommy doing a poor-but-very-fucking-loud impression at half five on a hung over morning is simply out of order. Freemo chased him to the back of the bus, head splitting as he did so. "Alright! Alright!" shouted Tommy, dodging the blows. "I'm fucking going!"

Freemo slumped back into his seat, putting a comforting arm around his wife as they tried to blot out the strains of a Cockney knees-up from the back of the bus. The dozing couple were soon awoken though, as the video screens on the coach hissed into life. They opened their weary eyes to see what was happening.

There, on the screen not five feet from them, was the raunchiest blue movie that Julie (if not Freemo) had ever seen.

Freemo gave up, to cackles of laughter from the lads at the back of the bus. Julie stared out of the window, disgusted. Freemo searched for (and found) the beer Tommy had offered him earlier. And he broke into song as he started on his free breakfast. Fair play. Even the isolated Bradley joined in.

At this time Shaun owned an off licence business in Worcester and it stocked the lads favourite beer – Banks's. Never one to miss a trick, Shaun had a few cases on board and was flogging it to the lads at a pound a can.... well, it was something of a captive market!.

As the coach speeded up towards London the sun came up; the movies turned from blue to grey and the lads lost interest.

Two stops in London and the coach was on its way to Dover. There were now over 40 lads on board, it was lunchtime and all was going well.

The coach arrived at Dover's East docks in plenty of time for the mid-afternoon ferry, so they parked up and went in search of the nearest pub. And they found it, complete with a pool table and darts, just a few hundred yards away.

Grisly, Coey and the London boys sat quietly drinking in a Tommy-free corner. The Wolverhampton boys attempted darts. Kidderminster took on Worcester at pool. Julie slept on the coach while the lads happily drained three or four beers. Tommy strummed away to himself.

Remarkably, they trooped back onto the bus at the agreed time – an hour before they were due to sail. No-one wanted to miss this game! Equally remarkably, no-one had forgotten or lost their passports and customs were satisfied very quickly. Shaun, sensing duty free prices on board, reduced his prices to 75 pence as the coach rumbled up the metal loading ramp and onto the ship. He sold his last few cans.

The lads had been warned by the driver to behave themselves on the ninety minute crossing. On earlier Spurs trips fighting had broken out mid-channel and the ship's ensign had 'gone missing'. Merchant ships can't dock without that ensign and so the Captain offered a 'blind-eye' armistice, otherwise threatening to turn the ship round and return to England. By some miracle, the ensign re-appeared and that ferry was able to dock, even though a handful of Spurs were nicked on arrival for the fighting.

In any case, the crossing was quick, calm and uneventful. Most of the lads passed it at the bar; a couple lost money at blackjack and two more spewed up. But uneventful.

As the lads re-boarded the coach, they found an exasperated driver blocking their way. "You CANT bring booze on the coach!" he worried. "I'm under orders from the Police! I'm going to have to search you all."

Easy enough. Freemo sent Julie on with the first bottle of vodka. No one was going to search her! He got on empty handed and allowed himself to be searched. Half a dozen others pushed and hassled the poor driver and as they did so, Freemo made his way to the back of the bus and threw open the emergency exit doors as the driver was distracted by the others. The lads quickly loaded their cases of Fosters lager and vodka onto the coach. Eventually the driver was convinced that no on had brought any alcohol on board and so, regulation complied with, he rolled off the ferry to unleash the lads on continental Europe.

Happily they made their way over the flat landscape to Brussels. Some had remembered to adjust their watches and some hadn't.

The blue films had been replaced by Tottenham videos of past European glories – wonderful days and nights against Milan, Wolves, Benfica…. every Spurs goal was cheered. Freemo was wide awake by now.

So, with twenty four hours until kick off, the bus arrived on the outskirts of the Belgian capital. No-one had bothered to book a hotel – some reckoned they would stay up all night but most decided that they would need to get their heads down for a few hours. A plan was needed.

The driver was becoming impatient and asked the lads what they wanted to do. Those on the coach had differing amounts of money to spend. The general consensus was to head for the red light district in north Brussels – beers and hotels would be cheaper there. And so the poor driver navigated his way through the post rush hour traffic, past the huge Stella Artois building and into the seedier part of town.

Whilst he was doing this, the lads had snapped into gear. No hotel was going to let forty some pissed Spurs fans in – especially as the news was showing that there had been a football related shooting in the area the previous night. Apparently, a Tottenham fan named Flannagan had been in some sort of a row with a Belgian bar owner and left without paying. The fella followed him into the street, pulled a gun and shot him dead. Feelings were running extremely high – not only amongst Spurs fans but also amongst the locals who were understandably afraid of repercussions.

Flemish and French are the languages used in Brussels. No-one had a chance with Flemish, but both Tommy and Freemo spoke passable French. Which is why they found themselves pushed to the front as the lads entered the reception area of the modest hotel they had been evicted from the bus at. The coach driver had told them he would be leaving at midnight the next day and either from the place he had dropped them or an hour earlier from outside the ground.

The hotel receptionist looked very wary of the assembled mob as the allocated two stepped forward and into their best, most persuasive French.

"Vous etes Anglais?" queried the lady behind the desk. And without waiting for a reply added "No Spurs here" in perfect English. Freemo could clearly hear Grisly muttering "Fuck 'em – lets all go on the piss" rather too loudly as he went into lie mode. He had a quick look around and no-one was showing any colours.

"Nous ne sommes pas Spurs", he smiled, waving his arms furiously as he explained in Franglais that the lads were, in fact, a touring football team who would take any accommodation they could get as those hooligans from London were in town.

Tommy chimed in his support at just the right moments and the hotelier began to visibly waiver. Freemo noticed and was in like a flash. "And we will, d'accord, pay you in cash in advance" he declared, producing a large wad of cash and slapping it loudly on the counter. That did it – they were in! It was nearly eleven o'clock at night, but they were in! But his Freemo's and Tommy's passports were taken as security.

72

The lads were shown the various available rooms and split fairly naturally into sharing groups of friends. Freemo made sure he and Julie, the only girl on the trip, had a double en-suite room, then the others worked out who would sleep where easily and quickly.

The Londoners doubled or trebled up, as did the Wolverhampton contingent and the others. Some had single rooms (lucky lads); some got twins (ditto); some doubles (not so) and some were in family rooms. Some were en-suite; some had to share a bathroom along the corridor. The rooms were clean though.... and they were in!

It was late now and most of the Spurs were knackered. The combination of a very early start and so many beers had taken its toll. A few – a very few – turned in straight away. The rest were disorganised and disappeared off in various directions in their own little groups. Some looked for a late bar; some wanted something to eat. A couple went looking for 'women of the night'. Freemo and Julie opted for drinks and a snack in the hotel's bar – Stella was the same anywhere, after all!

The lads awoke next morning in various stages of inebriation or hangover. The spreading news of the Spurs fan who had been shot dead, coupled with dehydration and stonking headaches set a bad tone for the day.

Freemo, Julie and Tommy breakfasted early – they wanted to check out and recover their precious passports in case of any trouble.

These three sat together, near the only window in the dingy basement dining room, forcing the odd croissant down to try to soak up the beer. Swigging strong coffee to wash them down. As they ate and carefully balanced their aching heads in their trembling hands, a few more of the lads wandered in. The news wasn't great....

Graham and Pete had got into a bicycle fight within seconds of leaving the hotel the previous night. Graham caught one in the mouth but luckily no-one was seriously hurt. A few more lads happened along and the dining room began to fill up. All were listening intently to the chain fight story when "WHUUUUUUMMMPPP!". Incredibly, a bed flew

73

past the dining room window and smashed into small pieces in the courtyard outside.

"What the fuck's THAT all about?", Tommy asked, worriedly glancing at Freemo.

"Well…" started one of the Londoners, "… it's Grisly. He was happy enough with our room until he found out Coey had a shower, so he's ripped it off the wall and was trying to install it in our wardrobe. There just wasn't room, what with the bed and all…."

Freemo and Tommy had heard enough. They shot straight to reception with a bemused Julie trailing in their wake. Politely thanking the hotel for a lovely stay, the three checked out, recovered their passports and left VERY quickly, leaving the others to face the music. Perhaps these fuckers had guns too!

It was still early – not much after eight – and the Tottenham three found themselves out in the cobbled Brussels streets. Not knowing quite what to do, they decided to drop into a convenient bar to form a plan. Just far enough away from the hotel and round a corner or two. The ubiquitous Stella sign in the window had swung it for them and they barged ill-temperedly through the wooden door in the empty café bar.

The beers were only served in small glasses, but each one was only about fifteen pence. Result! And a couple of glasses later they were even beginning to enjoy the taste and feel half human again. They hadn't managed much breakfast but the barman gave them a don't-push-you-fucking-luck look when they asked for food. So Stella it was then.

The three all had their backs to the door and were a little surprised as familiar voices crept in. It seemed the bar was a little obvious after all. One-by-one, most of the coach party arrived at the back street bar. Tommy and Freemo's round had bulked out to ten drinks and other, similar sized, groups kept the barman smiling.

At those prices, many of the lads didn't want to move and so the day wore lazily on with them happily drinking, playing cards and beginning to talk about that night's match. It was only the first leg and so defeat wasn't the end of the world. A draw would be a good result – particularly if Spurs could get an away goal. And a win would make it all over. The Anderlecht fans were no worry, so the lads didn't reckon on too much trouble.

Tommy and Freemo decided they weren't getting pissed enough and so opted to add a double Pernod for each of them whenever either of them bought their round. They got more and more pissed as the day wore on – still in the same bar. The barman periodically produced a few nibbles to keep them there – and it worked like a charm.

As afternoon began to turn into evening some of the group decided it was time to make a move towards the ground. After all, they had been in that one bar for nearly ten hours! A large group left for the ground. It included Julie, but not Freemo who was by now 'a little confused'.

It was not until a little while later that a very pissed Freemo realised he had lost his partner. But wasn't the main problem. The fact that she had his fucking match ticket was. Bollocks! Tommy and Shaun were there to comfort him as he burst into tears, convinced he was going to miss the game. Shaun even offered Freemo his own ticket – what a mate!

Too much being enough, they mopped up their drinks, thanked the landlord and attempted to negotiate the tram system to the ground. And – amazingly – they managed to arrive over half an hour before kick off. Better still (and by complete chance), there by the tram stop was Julie! After ensuring that she still had his ticket, Freemo hugged his long lost partner.

And so they made their way onto the terraces reserved for the large Tottenham support – over five thousand fans had got tickets. Demand had been a lot higher, but the lucky five thousand massed on the terraces behind one goal, supplemented by maybe five or six hundred more in 'home' areas of the stadium.

Freemo didn't remember too much about the occasion... a purpley team.... a Paul Miller goal..... a bandage swathed Paul 'Ol at half time…. a one-all draw…. lots of singing….. the feeling of a job well done….. an awful second half headache.

Apparently young 'Ol had got into some sort of barney, had cut his head and had ended up being tended to at the hospital – hence the head bandage.

In any case, the lads happily, drunkenly spilled out of the ground….. and straight into a mini riot. A few locals had decided to have a go and the travelling Tottenham contingent had turned nasty. Not stopping at just chasing off the aggressors, they started rocking and overturning parked cars. One was set on fire. The riot Police moved in and a few gas canisters were set off to quell the trouble.

Things were getting really nasty as the lads coach pulled into the appointed meeting place.

The Police were – just – managing to contain the riot as the lads piled back on to their coach. Worry lines had appeared on the driver's face. Surely his hair was a little greyer? The driver was understandably anxious for a quick get away and insisted on a rapid head count.

"Forty two, forty three…. Nope. One missing" said Bradley. Bollocks! Who was missing? Mates checked mates, but the inevitable problem was Grisly. "Well" retorted the purple faced driver "if he isn't back in five fucking minutes then we're off without him."

A few of the lads went back on to the streets in an effort to find him, but with no luck. Just as the driver's patience was at the end of its tether, up the bus steps stumbled a bedraggled Gris. He held his arms out for silence.

"Lads", he proclaimed irrelevantly, "I have an announcement to make. Sorry driver – I won't be more than a second or two.

The busload hushed as Grisly dramatically cleared his throat.

"I have to tell you" he began in Churchillian tones, "that I am becoming a Belgian citizen. I shall, of course, still support England in the football, but I'm going to stay and live here in Belgium".

"Fuck off Gris – you're pissed! Sit down!" the lads chorused

Grisly motioned for silence again. "No lads. Seriously. I met this girl last night and I love her. I'm only here to collect my bag".

At this, the lads jumped him, trying to hold him down until the bus had got under way. They grabbed his jacket, but Grisly managed to slip out of it and hop off the bus back into the Belgian night.

"Oh fuck him", someone said. And the rest muttered agreement. So the bus, with Grisly's passport, his money and his change of clothes, set off home without him.

On the return ferry crossing the lads all bought the next day's papers. A bit about the riot, but mostly positive stuff for once. One headline made the lads laugh "Now pay me what I'm worth" from Paul Miller. He was due a pay cut then!

As the coach wound its way back – via London – to Gloucestershire, there was only one further incident of note. Someone punched the increasingly annoying Tommy. His guitar was now down to just two intact strings. Everyone was hung over and tired. And STILL he persisted with his cheery Chas and Dave songs! Well, he deserved punching.

Result : Anderlecht 1 – 1 Tottenham Hotspur (Miller)

Attendance : 40,000

FOOTNOTE: Spurs next game – the following weekend – was away at Manchester United. Somehow, Grisly had got back with no passport and no money. There he was, large as life, on the Old Trafford terraces.

Oh and by the way...

~

In 1982, Tottenham successfully retained the F.A. Cup – exactly as they had done twenty years earlier - when they beat their opponents, Queens Park Rangers, after a replay.

Once again Freemo's boss came up trumps for him with two great seats for the first game, which he and his wife gratefully used. He had also given two to two colleagues.

The game wasn't going as expected as the unfancied Rangers had managed to hold Spurs 0 - 0 in normal time.

It remained that way until, with only ten minutes of extra time remaining, Glenn Hoddle hit a twenty yard shot which deflected in off Tony Currie. Ecstatic, Freemo turned left instead of right in his celebrations. And to this day it's the only time he's kissed a bloke with a beard.

But Q.P.R. managed to net an equaliser through Terry Fenwick with under five minutes to go and so a replay – only the third in F.A. Cup final history, proved necessary.

Smiffy could only get a ticket in the Q.P.R. end. Some 'wag' there held up a dead chicken. Smiffy sneered. And got his nose broken (yet again).

Ultimately Spurs won with another Hoddle goal – a penalty after Graham Roberts was brought down.

They had won the cup. On May 27th – Freemo's birthday.

~

CHAPTER SIX

EVERTON AWAY
ARSES ON FIRE
(25/8/1984)

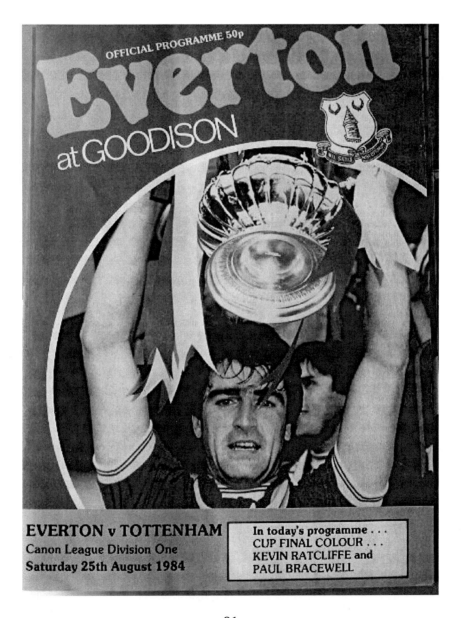

Freemo, Smiffy, Lesley and Julie had passed a happy summer fortnight in the Algarve. Lots of sunshine and Sagres. On their return home, Freemo found – amongst all the credit card bills – an envelope with a Liverpool postmark. Should be the tickets for the season's opener at Everton. He impatiently pulled at the envelope and sure enough there were the four tickets he had requested. As always, Spurs had sold out their allocation and so Freemo rang the Everton ticket office. He claimed that the four were 'neutrals' – neither Everton nor Spurs – and that they just wanted to take in the game whilst in the area. He explained that, as the girls were going to be present, they needed tickets in a safe area of the ground – and that they didn't mind paying a little bit extra for the privilege.

And now these tickets had arrived – four seats in the very front row of the main stand. Yahoo! Yes, they were expensive by northern club standards but they certainly looked good seats. And the price should keep the scally street urchins out.

Freemo wasted no time in calling Smiffy with the good news. There were things to do. Jim had a car to hire and had to ensure he was off work that Saturday. Lesley too. But these details were easily sorted and Smiffy duly sounded the car horn outside Freemo's at just after eight on match day.

Because it was a 'couples' day the lads were a lot better behaved than normal. No late night piss up on the Friday. No trip to Sainsburys to fill the boot up with beers for the journey. No farting contest. Anyhow, Smiffy still had a dodgy tummy after the Portuguese Cataplana so it would have been highly dangerous for all concerned. And Freemo didn't believe women should fart anyhow. So it was a subdued journey up the motorway. Freemo glanced furtively at his watch until it was ten-thirty and then pronounced that he desperately needed a piss. (just after they had passed a motorway service area). Smiffy cottoned on very quickly and swung the car off the M5 at the (highly convenient) next exit.

The lads were dreading a Little Chef or a petrol station with toilets, but as luck would have it the first building they came to was a pub! An open pub! Result. The lads jumped out of the car. In his haste Smiffy even clicked the central locking before the girls could get out of the car, got a bollocking and had to go back and do it properly.

Freemo rushed ahead to the bar and by the time the others had caught him up was already in possession of a lager and a lager top for Jim. "What would you like, ladies?" he asked, smiling.

"I thought you were desperate for the loo Freemo" remarked Lesley. "You must think we're bloody daft!".

"Must be all that sitting down" replied Freemo weakly. "I felt better when I stood up". In any case he took a couple of big swigs and disappeared to the Gents to pretend to piss. Well, it seemed only polite in the circumstances.

The couples got on well – Freemo and Smiffy were good mates and their partners knew them well enough by now not to be fooled by little tricks like this. They were always at it. The girls got on well enough with each other too. They could compare notes on who was the biggest bastard.

One round turned quickly into three. The fruit machine got its morning feed. Someone had told Freemo that the best time to play them was on a Saturday or Sunday morning at opening time. They only pay out a percentage of what had been put in and fruit machines are often filled by pissed up people on a Friday or Saturday night. In any case, the theory hadn't worked that day. Aware of the passing time, they filed back out to the car park and set about finishing their journey.

It was raining quite hard as they arrived in Liverpool. Smiffy kerb-crawled round the back streets looking for a place to park where the car wouldn't be burgled. The car had locking wheel nuts for the alloy wheels. No hub caps to worry about. Before long he found a space in a street of terraced houses – not too far from the ground. It looked quiet enough. But as they locked the car a little girl – she could only have been four or five – emerged, holding one of those useless kiddies plastic umbrellas. "Mind you car, Mister?" she asked, holding out her tiny wet hand.

"Fuck off out of it!" was Smiffy's first reaction. But Freemo spotted two or three ten to twelve year old lads in the shadows. The ones who would run keys down the bodywork or snap the wing mirrors or aerial off if they weren't well paid. Sighing, Freemo fished a couple of quid out of his pocket and handed it to the girl.

"It's five quid around here, Mister" she said, without any hesitation.

"And you're definitely going to stay here and look after our car until we get back in four hours?" Freemo asked.

"Yes, Mister. Definitely Mister", she didn't miss a beat and smiled sweetly.

"Well then I'll pay you the other three quid when we get back and make sure the car's not been touched. OK?"

The toddler seemed to know when she was beaten. OK Mister" she replied. "But don't be later than six. Me Mam gets me tea ready for six". She toddled off in her pink PVC Sou' Wester and handed the spoils over to the older lads.

"Last we see of her!" they joked as they made their way towards the ground, looking for a safe drinker en route.

It was raining harder now. All the pubs they had passed so far had been full of murderous looking Evertonians and they hadn't chanced it.

Smiffy suddenly spotted the official Everton Supporters Club and wondered if they might be able to get in. Freemo was a life member of the Spurs Supporters Club – they gave you a card with a big red stripe on it and a choice of a large or small oval badge. Anyhow, all the supporters clubs were affiliated and, even though he had long ago lost his membership card, Freemo managed to convince the old fella on the door to sign them in for the day.

Once inside and in the dry, jackets exchanged for a raffle ticket in the cloakroom, they took a look round at the facilities.

It was exactly what you might expect in any working mans club anywhere – sticky wooden floor, hard chairs and formica tables. A small stage with a microphone and one of those bingo-ball-tumbling contraptions. Smelly toilets. Very few women. Supporters with scarves. A small TV showing football previews with the sound turned down. Half a dozen busy fruit machines with larger than average jackpots. A large fag machine. Blue smoke hanging in the lights. A long queue at the bar. At least ten middle aged men wearing 'Steward' badges like proud school prefects.

But it was warm and dry. It sold beer. Remarkably cheaply. And so the four settled quietly in a corner, straining to listen to the TV. They blew their cover by ordering lager. All the locals drank mild or bitter it seemed. So why have a fucking lager pump then?

They even managed to dry out and read the two soggy match programmes they had picked up on the way. And the hour or so until they had to brave the elements again and walk the remaining short distance to the ground passed quickly. Happily. The lads were expecting big things from Tottenham this season. In fact they expected big things every year, but the hopes had always dissolved away by the start of October. But this was the very first game of a new season an so, dreams intact, the four recovered their still damp coats and stepped past the doorman out into the wet, now busy, street.

Of course none of the four had worn colours and – as they weren't drinking lager – they mingled easily into the crowds. Freemo had sussed out where they had to go whilst still in the supporters club. No point in giving the game away by asking for directions.

It was only a five minute walk, but the summer rain seemed harder than ever now as they neared Goodison Park. Once the turnstiles had been negotiated and token searches endured, the four regrouped under the cover of the main stand. There were now only five minutes until kick off and so they immediately began to make their way up to the top level. The top tier of Everton's main stand is very steep. It feels like you would fall over the front if you stumbled. There were even escalators to take you up there. All in all, the lads were quite impressed.

On arriving at the back of the top tier, one of the Everton stewards pointed vaguely down the steep stairs. "Front row. On the left" he offered.

They carefully picked their way down to the front row and turned left towards their seats. Freemo was at the front, checking seat numbers as they went.

When they eventually located the correct seats, they found six scousers sitting in those four seats. Maybe aged fifteen or so. Not very big.

"Excuse me lads" Freemo said "these four are our seats". The scallies exchanged bored glances and squashed a bit closer together, freeing up two of the four seats.

"No lads" Freemo persisted "we have paid for four seats. These four. Please can you go back to your own seats?".

"Bollocks la'". "Fuck off back to London". "Here lads, we've got some Cockney wankers in". "Your fucking problem la'". These were the politest of the replies.

So Freemo did the only thing he could think of and called the steward over. The steward DID make the scousers move, but the teenagers were not best pleased. They moved to seats directly behind the lads and proceeded to make all the bigger Evertonians in the stand aware that the four were "Cockney twats", whilst loudly mocking Freemo by shouting "Steward! Steward!" in high pitched girlie voices. As if he'd told teacher on them.

The front of the main stands top tier is pretty close to the tier below. And wouldn't you know, this tier was populated by a large mob of Everton hooligans who could, it seemed, almost jump up and reach them. Fucking perfect!

The displaced teenagers lost no time in pointing out the four to the mob below. Things were pretty hairy but calmed down a little when the game kicked off and football diverted at least SOME of the aggression.

You can always trust Spurs. They scored four fucking goals that day! To say it didn't help the mood of the locals was something of an understatement!.

They set fire to Smiffy's arse by emptying two boxes of matches under his seat and then throwing a lighted one into the pile.

The mob below held up a Stanley knife and promised to cut off Freemo's ears at full time. Everyone had to use the same exit to get out into the street.

"Hope we don't fucking score again!" muttered Smiffy, rubbing his arse. The lads had to do something. And quickly. They developed a whispered plan. Leave early. Wait until Everton were on the attack and then leg it up the stairs and out. Freemo worried that Everton might never attack, but it was all they had. The girls were made aware and so, in a rare Everton attack, fifteen minutes before the final whistle, the besieged four legged it to the back of the stand. One lad at the front, one at the rear. Girls in the middle for some sort of protection.

Smiffy and Freemo had been certain that they would be followed out. By some miracle they weren't and they managed to get out of the ground and on to the streets outside without incident. That's where the plan ran out of steam.

They were split between trying for the car and a quick getaway or holding out for an hour until the mobs had dispersed. Annoyed Everton fans leaving early made up their minds for them. They made a dash for the sanctuary of the Everton Supporters Club, only to be greeted by a locked door! They hammered furiously on the glass at the dozing doorman, who simply pointed to his watch to indicate that they would be opening in another ten minutes.

But the looks on the lads faces; the presence of two scared looking girls; the persistent rain – who knows, but one of them made him relent. He half opened the door to ask what the problem was and that was enough. Freemo barged through the gap and let the others in.

"Sorry mate, but you'd better lock it. Fucking quick!" he said as they apologetically picked up the doorman from the sticky carpet. He locked the main door and they dusted him down, explaining the urgency of getting themselves off the street.

The doorman was old-school. Disgusted by his own fans treating visitors in that way. He even opened the bar early by way of an apology. A geezer.

Safe now, with drinks in hand, their senses of humour began to return.

"How's your arse, Jim?" Freemo quipped.

"Fuck off! I can't hear you. I've only got one ear" came the almost instant reply.

FOOTNOTE : Spurs ran out easy 4-1 winners of the game. The lads returned to the car about six o'clock and – their surprise – out popped a soaking wet little five year old in a pink Sou' Wester. Clutching an inside out plastic umbrella. She had been there for over four hours. "Hello Mister" she smiled. "I stopped them bad boys scratching your car" she said disarmingly. The lads fished out a soggy fiver and pressed it into her sodden little hand, "Now bugger off home for tea before you get in trouble with your Mum!" The happy youngster splashed in all the puddles as she ran home.

Result : Everton 1 – 4 Tottenham Hotspur (Falco, C. Allen (2),
Chedozie)

Attendance : 35,630

Oh and by the way...

~

As the result of an accident at work, Spence managed to cut off the top joint of his index finger. Luckily for him it wasn't on the hand he used to write with.

But that's not what the compensation tribunal believed. After numerous interviews, they tossed him a pen to sign the damages agreement.

Spence had developed wonderfully scrawny hand-writing with his normal hand and signed in a spider like script.

The arbitrators sighed and paid him out.

Spence's handwriting improved dramatically very shortly after that meeting!

~

CHAPTER SEVEN

SUNDERLAND AWAY
FULL OF BEANS
(4/9/1984)

Freemo worked hard all day and skipped lunch so he could leave early. Tottenham were playing Sunderland that night and he planned to drive up after work. His wife Julie couldn't leave early and so he was travelling up there on his own. Freemo reckoned it was about a one and a half hour drive if he timed it right and missed the rush hour traffic in Bradford and Leeds, so at four-thirty he made his excuses and headed for the car, taking his tie off as he walked across the car park on a blustery Tuesday afternoon. Mind you, the car park at Grattan was blustery even in the middle of Summer.

It was still early season and Spurs had started off well. After three games they had beaten Everton away, drawn at home with Leicester (a disappointment) and then followed up with a home win versus Norwich. And so at this stage they were flying high. Sunderland were never deemed too much of a threat, even at Roker Park, and Freemo was very hopeful of another victory to cement their position at the top of the table as he set out on his journey.

The Bradford traffic was not yet a problem and Freemo cut across country a little to avoid the Leeds ring road's rush hour congestion. In no time, he was heading North on the A1.

Scotch Corner came and went and Freemo forked off for Sunderland. He looked at his watch – still well before six and so he pulled into an inviting looking pub car park for a quick drink.

He had brought along a coat, a jumper and a pair of trainers and so he quickly folded his jacket into the boot, pulled on the warm jumper – it was noticeably chillier here than in West Yorkshire, even though they weren't too far apart – and changed his shoes.

Freemo went into the pub's lounge with the folded newspaper he had nicked from work under his arm. Very useful if you just wanted to sit anonymously in the corner of a hostile pub. Or if you needed a dump. Freemo could never understand how women could visit the loo without something to read. Uncivilised, somehow.

In any case, this wasn't a hostile pub. It was in the middle of nowhere and the wind gusted across the small car park as he pushed forward into the hospitable pub. Inside a warm fire glowed in the hearth, despite it being only early September. The sort of pub that could make Freemo late for the game.

He ordered as pint and plonked himself in a chair near the fire. The lounge bar was nearly empty at this early hour. Not much in the tabloid – decent tits on page three. A bit of football gossip. A small column previewing tonight's match. The Sunderland team was likely to include Barry Venison, Chis Turner and Clive Walker. Turner, their diminutive keeper, was apparently in top form so far this season. The preview reflected on the previous meeting at Roker between the two teams, that same April, when they had fought out a 1 – 1 draw. It seemed Sunderland were confident too.

Freemo finished his pint, looked at his watch again and ordered another. He had to gulp it down, though, as time was passing all too quickly.

He set out again soon after and hit the outskirts of Sunderland at about a quarter to seven. The floodlights guided him towards the stadium and he parked up at what he reckoned might be a safe distance. Far enough away to avoid attention from hostile locals – things could sometimes get a bit naughty when you visited the north east – but close enough to be able to easily arrive in time for kick off. With MAYBE enough time for a quick pint in a handy pub.

Paper tucked under safely under his arm, he put anything remotely valuable in the boot, locked the car and set out towards the distant floodlight pylons.
All the pubs he passed seemed full to overflowing with neanderthal looking Sunderland fans, so Freemo gave them a miss. He discarded the paper - it could be of no use now – and continued on until he reached the ground.

The next problem was to locate the away fans turnstiles without blowing his cover. There were gangs of home fans seemingly roaming the streets looking for stragglers just such as him. He bought a programme and began reading the Sunderland news pages as he walked. That should fool them!

As always seemed to be the case in these circumstances, he had turned the wrong way and ended up walking almost an entire lap of the ground before locating the Tottenham entrance. And that meant walking through queuing mobs of pissed up northerners singing their war songs. He couldn't even say 'excuse me' as he had to push through. The accent, or lack of it, would give him away immediately.

And so he pushed on and hoped. As luck would have it he made it through unscathed and undiscovered. It just SEEMS like everyone is staring at you when you are in that situation, but in actual fact you are almost invisible if you do the right things.

A relieved Freemo walked past the Police cordon and joined the queuing Spurs fans. Because it was a cold, north eastern Tuesday night; an unattractive opponent; a very long journey; Spurs had played three days before; there were no trains home until the next morning... a variety of reasons.... the travelling support from London was not huge. Perhaps eight hundred to a thousand die hard fans had made the trip to Roker Park.

Freemo saw a few familiar faces and for geographical reasons a larger than normal proportion of them were northern Spurs. Tommy from Lincoln, Sget from Grantham, The Warrington Micks – they had all turned out. There were also the usual suspects from London. Freemo greeted them all warmly. It was great to be back amongst your own!

On entering the stadium all fans were fairly thoroughly searched for anything that could be deemed an offensive weapon. Penknives. Metal combs – that sort of thing. Entrance was held up because of this and there was no time to get a beer from the stand under the terracing.

Tottenham fans had been allocated a pitch side enclosure on the side of the ground this year. They were in an area which stretched either side of the half way line, with a large area of 'no-mans-land' – perhaps twenty five to thirty yards of empty terracing - at either end. The Sunderland fans were housed in the large terrace to their right.

The teams were announced and the away fans cheered the announcement of each of their players names and then began working through their list of songs. They had a unique one for each member of the team.

The Sunderland fans seemed a little subdued that evening and the crowd was only small by their standards. Even the 'Roker Roar' sounded tame as the teams took to the field.

The teams were pretty much as predicted by the tabloid and neither team appeared to have any absentees through injury.

The game kicked off smack on seven thirty, but, after an initial flurry of activity, it soon settled into a cagey, not too many risks affair.

The first half was a big disappointment. Tottenham had probably just shaded it, but Turner, their tiny goalkeeper, had managed to save anything that came at him. Not that there was much. 0 – 0 was more than either side deserved.

The bored Sunderland fans began baiting their cockney bastard opponents. The equally bored Londoners replied to their dirty northern bastard opponents. Feelings had begun to rise quite high.

As Freemo turned back to watch the game there was an almighty thud from right behind him. He jerked round and there on the terrace step behind him, was a small can of Heinz baked beans. The Wearsiders were using their fucking shopping as missiles! A can of beans, thrown from thirty yards, could seriously injure – maybe even kill - someone if it hit their head. The line of Police had seen it, but they simply laughed to one another as more missiles began to rain down. They didn't appear to have too much time for cockney bastards either.

Freemo moved a couple of paces to the left and got back to watching the game. Spurs had stepped up a gear after the interval and were mounting wave after wave of attacks on the Sunderland goal. But every shot, every header, from every angle seemed to be saved by Chris Turner. He probably had one of his best games ever that night as he almost single handedly kept Sunderland in the game.

And then, of course, it happened. Sunderland broke away and won a penalty. West stepped up and scored it. From that point on, Sunderland were intent on shutting up shop. Tottenham redoubled their efforts and pushed defenders forward into midfield; midfielders forward into attack. No prisoners.

Thunk!! Freemo winced in pain as he grabbed at his right collarbone. Through screwed up eyes he looked down and saw the large lump of lead which had caused the pain. He picked it up and turned it over in his hand – this was a heavy fishing weight, maybe four ounces – that had been thrown from the Sunderland fans.

Freemo was fucking furious. He ran to the edge of no-mans-land, intent on throwing it back. He noticed the close attentions of the watching constable just in time, so he changed direction, handed it to the Policeman and began remonstrating with him about the lack of protection or action to stop such lethal missiles being thrown. "Fuck off or you're nicked" was the reply. So he fucked off. Even further left this time, where he hoped the missiles couldn't reach. His shoulder was really very sore but he didn't want to make too much fuss in front of his mates.

On the pitch, Tottenham's renewed efforts were still being thwarted by the Sunderland keeper. How could someone so fucking small command his box so well? He was catching everything too, not merely punching. Some of the saves were unbelievable.

And because of him, Sunderland held on to win. Tottenham's solid start to the season was over.

As they left the ground, Freemo toyed with the idea of complaining to the Police about the missiles. Surely the Sunderland fans had had to be searched on their way into the ground too? (But would a can of baked beans be deemed an offensive weapon?). Those two missiles, if they hit someone in the temple, could definitely kill. But the Police had just laughed. He decided that, if he DID complain, he was very likely to be nicked and get a kicking in the cells anyhow and so in the end he didn't bother.

Freemo trudged back to the car nursing a sore shoulder. Very pissed off. The Sunderland fans had quickly dispersed back into the pubs. Or back home for their tea. Fucking beans no doubt!

There was no trouble outside. The bulk of the Tottenham fans were escorted back to the nearby coach and car park by mounted Police. Freemo had to go in the opposite direction, but it didn't feel threatening.

Safely back at the car, Freemo started out for home in Skipton –using a slightly different route from the outward trip from Bradford. He ignored the temptation of the welcoming pub he had enjoyed on the way up and got a lot nearer home before stopping for a couple of lagers before last orders.

He got home later than expected and got a bollocking. He was sober. Spurs had lost. His shoulder had started throbbing.

All in all it had been a really shit day.

Result : Sunderland 1 – 0 Tottenham Hotspur

Attendance : 18,895

Oh and by the way...

~

After hearing of the Warwickshire vs. Worcestershire Spurs challenge match in the 1970s, the Lincolnshire Spurs laid down a challenge to the Worcester lads.

A full coach load of players met as agreed outside the Perdiswell pub in Worcester. The Worcester lads were properly organised this time. They laid off the drink before the match, unlike their friends from the north.

Big Tom – he was over 6'6" – goaded Freemo. Tom was a centre half and Freemo a centre forward. Tom was confident that he could stop Freemo from scoring. So confident that he bet beers on it.

The match kicked off on one of the many municipal pitches on the one-time aerodrome that was Perdiswell.

In the first minute, Pete Buzz slipped the ball inside to Freemo – they had played a lot of football together and had a good understanding. Freemo dragged it past a half pissed big Tom and smashed it into the net. 1 – 0. Beers sorted.

After another few minutes, a long raking ball to Vulch was deftly headed down for Freemo to tuck it inside the far post from outside the box. The combination had worked again. It was 5 – 1 as the lads tucked into half time oranges.

At one stage as Freemo bore down on goal, Sget (in goal) came out to challenge. Freemo headed the ball over him. Sget's flat cap fell over his eyes. Freemo collapsed on the floor laughing, an open goal at his mercy. Sget got up, picked up the ball, and carried on with the game.

Lincoln mounted a revival in the second half and got back to 5 – 4, but the Worcester lads stretched away again and ran out 9 – 4 winners. Freemo got 4. His brother Nige got two more.

~

CHAPTER EIGHT

HALIFAX AWAY – LEAGUE CUP
FLAT CAPS AND TV STARDOM
(25/9/1984)

Freemo rushed to finish early. His work was now based in Bradford and Spurs had drawn tiny Halifax Town in the early stages of the league cup. Halifax was only a few miles from where he worked and he wanted to have a few beers before the game. He left work at four and drove to pick up his wife, Julie. From there they drove for twenty minutes and soon arrived at the motorway turn-off which they needed.

Freemo swung the car into the car park of the modern-and-quite-expensive hotel adjacent to the motorway exit. He was, of course, still dressed in a suit and tie as he had had to travel straight from work.

The couple ordered drinks and commandeered two of the comfortable low armchairs in the hotel's lobby. Even though it was only late September, strong winds blew from the Pennines and there was already a definite chill in the evening air. And so the heat from the large flame-effect gas fire was very welcome. It was a good one, Freemo noted as he watched the fourth person in ten minutes idly toss their fag butt into the decorative flames.

The hotel obliged with bar snacks too – only a couple of bowls of chips and a toasted sarnie, but very welcome all the same. Freemo had had to skip lunch to be able to leave early. He hadn't eaten all day.

The snacks were washed down with strong lager, at least Freemo's were. It was only two miles to the Shay, where Halifax played. And Julie had agreed to drive home. Well, Freemo had driven there, and it was only fair to share the driving wasn't it?

The next time Freemo got up to go to the bar, he bumped into a smartly dressed man who happened to be passing. "Fucking hell mate!" he retorted instinctively. He was about to continue his tirade. Until, that is, he realised he was face-to-face with Mark Falco, the Tottenham striker. "Erm… Sorry Mark " he mumbled apologetically. "We're Spurs fans, here to watch the game. Knock in a few tonight mate!"

Mr. Falco smiled politely and continued on his way to the loo. Freemo was embarrassed. More so when he looked round the lounge and found the entire Tottenham squad looking over as they waited near the exit to board their team coach. Desperately wanting a set of autographs, but at the same time not wanting to intrude, Freemo decided against asking. Didn't have a pen or paper either.

As the team was only just leaving, he figured there should be plenty of time for another beer. Maybe even two, before they would have to brave the cold wind. And indeed one beer turned into two. With chasers. Freemo looked at his watch and sighed. Time to leave.

Julie took over the driving from there. A little more traffic was on the roads now, but it still wasn't too bad.

The Shay was a very small ground, holding only just over seven thousand fans. Even if every one of them drove, the traffic would be nowhere near as bad as for a Tottenham home game. And there was a big car park near the ground too. Julie parked up and the two walked the short distance on to the ground. It was beginning to get quite dark now and the floodlights were already on to guide them. Freemo had managed to get two front row seats in the main stand from Halifax as the Spurs allocation had again sold out very quickly.

They joined a queue of Yorkshiremen who sported thick, hairy overcoats and flat caps as they slowly shuffled forward to the turnstiles.

Halifax were a very small club and Tottenham were expected to win this game easily. Northern accented conversations bore out the concerns.

Freemo and Julie handed over the big bit of their tickets to the turnstile operator and retained the small part. They made straight for the pie and pint queue and again had to slowly shuffle forward, listening to more concerned Yorkshiremen's comments, muffled by the peaks of their caps.

A quick pint and they made their way down from the back of the stand to take their pitch-side seats. Freemo was none too pleased as he saw the makeshift scaffolding of a TV camera gantry obstructing his view of one goal. These were the most expensive seats in the fucking ground! He was not amused.

105

With only ten minutes to kick off, two hairy coats appeared at Freemo's side. "Excuse me young man" said one, "you are in our seats".

Freemo fumbled for his ticket stubs, inspected them and then triumphantly – sarcastically even – retorted "Look mate our tickets are Row A, Seats 103 and 104". He waved the stubs and pointed to the numbers on the back of their seats as he spoke. Confusion reigned as the two Yorkies also produced stubs with the same numbers on. "Fucking hell!" exclaimed a half pissed Freemo. "You must've bought fakes from a tout you pair of prats! We got ours direct from the club. "Aye, so did we lads" responded the flat caps. More confusion.

Freemo demanded to see their tickets. They LOOKED kosher enough. The Yorkshiremen, in turn, demanded to see his. They inspected Freemo's stubs carefully and then worried him by breaking into broad smiles.

"These are the correct seats, right enough" said one. "But you're in t'wrong stand lad. THAT'S the main stand over there!" he said, pointing to the stand on the opposite side of the pitch. Fuck it! With just over five minutes to kick off, Freemo managed to collar a donkey-jacketed steward and explain the problem.

"OK Sir. Don't worry – I'll walk you round the running track to your seats." He said helpfully. Freemo scrambled over the low wall and turned to help his wife over onto the orange running track.

The Shay, whilst being a small ground with poor, out of date facilities, is one fans tend to remember. An Acropolis like oval bowl of terraces and rickety stands. The bright orange running track between them and the pitch. Freemo thought they might have used it for greyhound racing. Or Speedway. Maybe both.

The pair were duly escorted round the track. As they passed the knot of Tottenham supporters behind and slightly to one side of the goal, Freemo hung back and milked the moment, giving a round of applause and several thumbs ups to the travelling support. They had come a long way and spent a lot of money getting to the game. They would struggle to get home. It was cold. Theirs would be a very late night and they would still have to work tomorrow. This was a good show.

The steward came back and hurried him along. They were about to walk past an opening in one corner of the terracing when donkey jacket put his arm out and stooped the couple from going any further. The fans erupted into cheers. Freemo couldn't understand why. Until, that is, the two teams started walking either side of him and his wife! They had only stopped at the mouth of the player's tunnel!

Freemo tried to shake hands with a few bemused Tottenham players. As Mark Falco passed, a half pissed Freemo shouted "Me again! Sorry about earlier Mark. Don't forget to knock a couple in!". Julie was highly embarrassed, particularly as she realised that the TV cameras were bound to be focused on them at that precise moment.

Once the teams had passed on to the pitch, the couple were allowed to continue the journey to their correct seats. Freemo was quite chuffed. He was almost old mates with Mark Falco by now!

Their seats were actually occupied and so, not wishing to create any more of a fuss – the match was already underway – they took up places in two empty halfway line seats about ten rows back.

The flat caps muttered annoyance as they moved through their ranks to the empty seats. "They're not even our fucking seats mate" snapped Freemo. Fuck 'em.

This was a two-legged encounter in the early stages of the League Cup. Even if Spurs didn't win emphatically tonight, Freemo was totally relaxed that they would finish the job off in the second leg at White Hart Lane. The Halifax fans – they all seemed like older men to Freemo – seemed to share his confidence. Halifax played at a low level AND they were having a poor season. On the other hand, Tottenham played at the top level. They had smashed Everton in the season's opener. It was only the fourth year of the decade and Spurs had already played in five Wembley finals (winning two FA Cups).

And then there was that John Chedozie chap. They had never seen anyone as fast as him. Every time he got the ball, Freemo laughed as they pulled their cap peaks down a little lower in one synchronised movement, muttering "Oh fucking hell, no! Not him again!" as the ball landed at Chedozie's feet and he set off at pace. "Faster than a fucking whippet that one!" remarked someone.

The match, unsurprisingly, went to form. Tottenham ran out easy 5-1 winners. Garth Crooks got a hat trick. And Freemo's new mate must have been paying attention – Mark Falco knocked in a couple too. John Chedozie ran riot that night and Halifax simply couldn't cope with his speed.

The capacity crowd – a little over 7,000 – cheered Halifax's consolation goal half-heartedly, but in truth their side had been well beaten. And they knew it.

Freemo and Julie made their way happily to the car park and were soon on the road home. The small crowd helped with the traffic.

Freemo decided he wasn't pissed enough and set about persuading his chauffeuse to stop at a pub on the way home. One with a TV. A TV which was showing the match highlights. And – surprise, surprise – he knew just the place. The couple settled into the red velour seats just as the extended highlights started.

As the teams came out, Julie cringed again. Her family had begun to take an interest in televised Tottenham games since Julie herself had. They were from London originally and one of her brothers had been on QPR's books for a while. So they were likely to be watching.

And there they were – larger than life. A besuited Freemo staggering around and annoying the team by trying to shake hands with everyone. With Julie tugging at his jacket in a vain attempt to hold him back.

"That's us that is!" a pissed Freemo pointed out to the packed pub. Julie cringed even more.

After the game finished – and three pints later, Julie managed to pour Freemo back to the car. They drove the rest of the way home in total silence. Freemo fiddled with the radio for something to do. He quickly lost interest and annoyingly left it half way between stations, blaring white noise into the car at high volume. Julie played a cassette. And turned the sound down. Freemo stared silently out of the window.

The next morning Freemo had a BAD hangover. He usually drank two pints of water and took two headache pills before going to bed, but he'd forgotten to do so this time. And Julie was in no mood to remind him.

He drove in to work, head throbbing after an Anadin breakfast, washed down with orange juice.

As he took his place at his desk, fifteen minutes alter than usual, one of his programming team called "Saw you on the tele last night Malc!".

"Get on with you fucking work " he snapped, kicking his office door firmly shut.

Result : Halifax 1 – 5 Tottenham Hotspur (Falco(2), Crooks(3))

Attendance : 7,027

Oh and by the way...

~

Stick was going on holiday. He asked Crowbar if he would nip into the house occasionally and turn on a few different lights.

Since the first time they had met, Stick didn't trust Crowbar. It somehow seemed that things went wrong around him. But everyone else had told Stick to fuck off and so he nervously entrusted Mick with the task.

"And PLEASE, Crowb., don't touch ANYTHING apart from the light switches" he pleaded as he left for the airport. "Don't worry mate. Leave things to me" replied his mate.

Now I'm not exactly sure why, but Crowbar decided it would be a good idea to turn the central heating back on the day before Stick returned home. And in normal circumstances that would have been thoughtful.

Mick flipped the switch on. The central heating groaned and then clunked ominously. And stopped working.

It cost Stick a few hundred quid to put right. To add insult to injury, Stick had hated Tunisia. He had been coerced into camel riding in the desert. He got the hump. Crowbar must be the unluckiest bloke in the world.

~

CHAPTER NINE

THE ITALIAN JOB
A HOLIDAY IN CATTOLICA
(mid 1980s)

It was just after the Christmas and New Year celebrations. Worcester was a good place to be at that time of year – numerous parties around Christmas and Fancy Dress pub crawls on New Years Eve.

But now it was all over, wasn't it? Isn't January a depressing time of year? Winter is at its coldest; the return to work; things are very flat after Christmas celebrations; the credit card bills starting to arrive... and nothing much to look forward to. Usually football trips made things less gloomy, but Tottenham had had a really poor spell so even Saturdays at the Lane weren't enough to lift the spirits.

The lads needed something to look forward to – an incentive to get out of bed on the freezing work mornings. And so a grumbly evening in the pub brightened up a great deal when someone suggested that the group of friends arranged a sunshine holiday for the summer.

Hollins, Crowbar, Smiffy, Spence and Freemo were in the White Hart that evening. They armed themselves with a few pints and sat down to start swapping ideas.

"I fancy Italy" said one. The others had no fixed ideas and so fell I with that. "Gonna need to be July – no football" chimed in another. "Who's going?" asked another and so they scrounged a pen and paper and started a list of definites, probables and maybes.

Hollins, Freemo (and Julie) were definites. Crowbar, Smiffy and Spence were 99% probables – they had to discuss it with their wives first. Up to nine probables already!

Three wifely confirmations were quickly made and now it was nine definites – off to somewhere in Italy, sometime in July. Things were taking shape nicely.

The nine arranged a pub meeting for the following weekend. The girls had collected a daunting set of holiday brochures and they set about sorting them into three piles:- No use whatsoever (too expensive); Might be OK (likely to be too expensive) and definitely interesting (ones they could afford).

They bickered just a little over which brochure went in which pile, but it was all friendly, constructive stuff over a few drinks.

Eventually the friends narrowed it down to three or four affordable choices. Some fancied Rimini, others Cattolica and still more Lido di Jesolo. Putting it to a vote, Cattolica won the day with five votes. So it was decided. Cattolica in July.

They looked at the weather. It was a bit better in late July. They looked at departure dates and found that if they wanted to fly on a weekend, they would need to leave from Luton. Some of the group had trouble getting a fortnight off work, midweek to midweek and so Luton it was then. Anyhow it wasn't that bad a drive – maybe a shade over two hours across country.

They looked at the accommodation options – they needed to be near a beach; near a few bars and eateries. And so they were able to narrow it down to their final choice – an apartment block in Cattolica, just across the port from the main beach. The necessary bars were there in the port, as were a handful of places to eat. And Cattolica itself was only a fifteen minute walk.

The decision now unanimously made, a preferred departure date was decided on and they set about costing this choice.

Nine travellers were proving difficult. Almost all apartments were for four or six and so either way they were going to be paying for three empty beds. Hmmmmm.

Stevie Brocks and postman Brian were at the bar – one a Mank and one West Ham, but hey! They were all friends. These two single guys lived mostly for the pub at that time and were quick and eager to sign up for what promised to be a boozy fortnight. Stevie Foster and Caroline declined the offer for work reasons.

Up to a total of eleven now, Hollins made a call to a guy he worked with – a lad named Kelvin. No one except Crowbar and Hollins knew him, but he was another Tottenham fan and a useful footballer too. His two colleagues half persuaded, half bullied him into it – Kelvin agreed on the spot and was invited down to meet everyone. Twelve was the magic number that made it cheaper for everyone and twelve had now signed up. Applications were now closed. Result!

Kelvin turned up and met the lads. He seemed a nice guy, if a little shy and maybe a bit gullible for the quick witted, fast mouthed friends.

Over the next two weeks, deposits were taken from everyone and the holiday was booked. Yahoo! The selected apartments each had two double bedrooms and two settees which converted to beds. There were four couples and four single lads – a perfect split. Couples would take the bedrooms; singles the settee beds. So now the only decision to make was which six went together in which apartment.

Of the singles, a natural split seemed to be Hollins and Kelvin (because they worked together and both supported Spurs) and Brian and Steve (because they were drinking buddies).

Of the couples the split seemed to be Freemo and Julie with Crowbar and Trish (the lads were both Thursday Night Married Men's Club members and Crowbar worked with Hollins and Kelvin); Spence and Pauline with Smiffy and Lesley (the couples had been friends for a long time).

Crowbar and Spence knew Steve and Brian well from the White Hart; Freemo and Smiffy were good mates with Hollins and so the two sixes were painlessly sorted.

Over the next few weeks the friends met regularly to chat about what they wanted from their holiday. The girls laid down a few token markers about not getting pissed every night and made vague mentions of 'cultural things', whatever they were. The lads nodded agreement whilst silently knowing very well that it was going to be one huge party.

An inter apartment football challenge sprung up from somewhere. No-one quite knew who first suggested it but it was very likely Kelvin or Freemo or Hollins. Their apartment had three very useful footballers in it. Freemo had been offered a trial with Worcester City of the Southern League (Conference level nowadays), Hollins had a trial at Oxford United (then a league team but also Conference level nowadays). And Kelvin was a good local level player.

In the other apartment, Brian and Brocksie were big lads who didn't play football. Spence had never played competitively. Only Smiffy was a good level local footballer. So why would THEY have made the challenge?

But they talked a bloody good game and, months in advance, a time was set (midnight) and a date (the middle Saturday of the holiday) for the grudge match.

All the lads enjoyed Banks's beer so Freemo promised to smuggle some out. To be donated to the winners. The lads in his apartment secretly agreed to pack yellow Spurs tops and blue shorts in their luggage too. A psychological advantage, even though they were confident it wouldn't be needed.

Winter turned quickly into Spring. Spring turned to Summer. Excitement grew. But the balance payment of the holiday was due and some of the friends weren't used to saving up for things. There were a few no-shows at meetings and a few worries as a result, but eventually everyone managed to come up with their share of the money on time. The balance was paid. Now they knew they were really off in just a few short weeks!

Postman Brian organised a minibus and driver to ferry the friends to and from Luton. It proved very cheap when the cost was shared by twelve.

The friends continued saving hard for their spending money. They had all discussed a figure as they all wanted to have roughly the same budgets as each other. No flash meals for some and burgers for the others on THIS holiday.

Currency was ordered and collected. They were all instant lira millionaires!

The week before departure seemed to drag on for ever, but finally the big day arrived. The minibus collected everyone and set off for Bedfordshire. Loaded with twelve holidaymakers and their luggage, it was all a bit of a squeeze. Some cases had to be sat on to fit everything in, but they just about managed. Thank fuck there weren't too many hills en route!

Just over two hours later the bus duly arrived at Luton's airport. Crowbar's wife, Trish, loved to organise people and no-one else gave a toss so it was she who collected passports and tickets from everyone, ready for check in. She who dragged the stragglers from the bar to the check in queue before they got too pissed. She who managed to book twelve seats 'together' on the plane. Round of applause. Once the friends reached the front of the queue, they had been informed of a two hour delay, due to 'operational reasons'. Great fucking start! The girls looked anxious. The guys raced for the bar. They began buying rounds of drinks in 'apartments'. The rivalry was building!

A further hours delay was announced. The lads shrugged. The girls sighed.

But eventually the friends were called to their boarding gate. Trish bullied everyone into line. The lads struggled to appear vaguely sober to the airline staff. Brian farted loudly as he boarded the plane.

The twelve settled into their seats – two complete rows of six with an aisle running down the middle of the plane. Freemo insisted on a window seat in case Brian farted all the way there. Even Trish smiled.

The trolley crew came round twice during the three hour flight. The lads ordered three drinks each time – a couple of beers and a short –

to keep up their fuel levels. Brocksie joined in the farting. Blaming cabin pressure. The neighbouring passengers (and some of the girls) were disgusted. Well, it is PRETTY anti social to fart on a plane isn't it? Lesley was hoping the oxygen masks might drop down.

"Fucking hell Steve! What have you been eating?" gasped Smiffy.

"Probably fucking sprouts" muttered the bloke four rows behind them. Row thirteen had apparently proved unlucky for him.

It was only a short haul flight and so there were no films to distract them. The cramped cabin conditions of the charter flight made it seem much longer than it actually was, but eventually they touched down, negotiated passport control (after instructions from Trish) and set up camp by the luggage carousel. They waited none-too-patiently for their cases to appear. Brian had managed to somehow free a load of luggage trolleys without using the usual coin required to separate them.

A short while later, the twelve friends emerged from the 'nothing to declare' channel and spilled out into the airport's arrivals hall. They quickly located their holiday rep – Thomson's holidays in this case - and were directed to the relevant transfer coach.

And only an hour and a half later the coach began dropping off holidaymakers in Cattolica.

The lads had, they now discovered, been allocated two apartments, but they were in two totally separate blocks. The rep assured them that the apartment blocks were within a few yards of each other, so they decided not to moan. Too much.

When the rep called for the first six from their group it didn't seem to matter much which six went and so Spence and co. took the first apartment. It was in a low rise block as opposed to the other one, which the rep pointed out, in a towering block just down the road.

Freemo and party were dropped there a couple of minutes later and – having checked in – made their way up to the seventh floor. Their apartment was at the end of a long marble corridor. They threw open the front door and found themselves in a comfy, modern lounge. Freemo and Trish agreed who would take each bedroom, cases were stashed and duty free bottles unloaded. Freemo gingerly opened his case – as promised he had stashed a seven pint can of Banks's bitter in there. He wasn't too sure if is would have exploded in the cold of the de-pressurised hold. But it looked to have survived fine – not even a dent. The large can was displayed in pride of place in their new lounge. Their apartment had balconies on two sides and had great views over the harbour and – in the middle distance – the blue Adriatic.

The twelve didn't bother unpacking that night. They simply met in the nearest harbour side bar which was still serving food and ordered themselves beers and hot dogs.

Now you may have gather that postman Brian was, in those days, a pretty basic, down to earth type of guy. He drank a lot; farted even more and preferred good, old fashioned English cooking. So you can imagine how pleased he was when the hot dogs eventually showed up. On toasted bread. With a salad garnish. Covered with French mustard.

"Oi! I ordered a fucking hot dog!" he shouted after the waiter. "And its taken nearly an hour to get here!". The waiter tried to explain that this was how hot dogs were served in Italy. Brian was adamant that he wasn't eating such foreign shit. He asked for it to be taken away, but snatched it back when he discovered that the kitchen had now closed for the night.

Brian spent the next ten minutes carefully discarding lettuce and then meticulously wiping every last bit of "fucking foreign mustardy stuff" from first the sausages and then from his toasted bread. Eventually he washed his hands and tucked in. "Now its fucking cold!" he moaned. Fucking hell Brian! He ate it anyhow.

The girls retired to bed early.

The other group of six were barely satisfied with their low rise apartment, but it was nowhere near as nice as the one in the tower block. Just clean and basic.

The lads stayed up late and finished the job of getting pissed. They amused themselves by watching the sneezing parrot on the perch outside the bar. "Fucking thing's on snuff" offered Crowbar as the bird sneezed loudly for the umpteenth time. And as the lads switched from beers to the house special 'Blue Lagoon' cocktails, Crowbar found he could do a passable impression of a snuff-fuelled parrot – something that was to resurface every day of the rest of the holiday.

Eventually, some time after two a.m., the eight lads went their separate ways. Freemo, Hollins and Crowbar decided on a late night dip. Kelvin thought they'd better not. Three of the four stripped down to their shreddies and jumped into the illuminated pool, splashing around happily (and noisily) for ten minutes whilst Kelvin sat in the shadows, worrying. The pool seemed very chlorinated and so the lads soon tired of it. They sat poolside for about ten minutes to dry off. And then set off in the lift, trousers in hand. All fell asleep immediately their head hit their pillows, though Hollins and Kelvin had to make up their beds on the couches first.

Morning arrived rather too soon. They had the welcome meeting to negotiate. And the girls wanted to organise a shop for breakfast provisions. The lads needed a few beers for the fridge. The group in the low rise apartment had now all seen the other one was much better and so decided to complain to the rep after the welcome meeting.

The twelve trooped into the meeting room early. Weak welcome cocktails were laid out, but no one else was there yet. Brian made a quick count. "Right lads – three each" he calculated. He downed three in three large gulps. The other lads followed suit. Then hid the empties behind the curtain and left the room again.

They rejoined the meeting just as the rep was quizzing a hotel worker about the missing drinks, sauntering in innocently and obviously blameless.

The apartment complainers were going to ask to see the rep – Frankie – privately, but were a little taken aback as she got the first punch in. She asked to see "the party of twelve at the back" after the meeting. The lads shuffled nervously and began to wonder how much to offer for the missing cocktails.

But the detention wasn't about that at all. The rep had had complaints from other guests about a noisy group "washing their trousers" (?) in the swimming pool at a ridiculously late hour. The lads could honestly tell her they had done no such thing. Anyhow, what WAS a sensible hour for washing fucking trousers in a swimming pool? "Why would we wash trousers on our first night?" said one. "All our stuff is still clean!". "And why in the swimming pool?" added another. "We have a washing machine!". Miserable bastards must've had too much vino was their conclusion. Frankie sighed resignedly and politely asked them to keep late night noise to a minimum. They, of course, agreed immediately.

The apartment complainers then made their point assertively and demanded one of a similar standard to their friends. The rep said that all Thomson's apartments in the area were full at the moment, but that she would review things if one became free. Fair enough. "Oh, any more of those cocktails left over?" asked Brian innocently as they left the meeting room.

The group soon found a small supermarket and bought bottled water, bread, eggs, cheese, tea, milk and coffee. Plus things the lads would never have thought of: washing up liquid, pan scourers, dishwashing cloths. The lads dutifully carried the shopping back. And then doubled back and bought the shed load of beer and mixers for the duty frees which they had not dared to pick up when the girls were around. Sorted, even if there wasn't QUITE enough room for all of them in either fridge.

The two groups decided to stay by their own pools for the first day but met up again in the shop for the third time shortly after. Apparently all swimmers – male of female – had to wear rubber swimming hats in the pool. Embarrassing. But the only way they could cool down. And so they bought the ones would they thought looked least embarrassing. All except postman Brian. His had pink flowers all over it.

Back by their respective pools and oiled up, Freemo's group happily sunbathed and swam. Spence had happened across from his group. The lads bought a football and the game of water cricket was soon invented. Running between the two sets of steps at the shallow end of the pool proved remarkably difficult. Crowbar threw in the occasional parrot sneeze for effect.

It was during one of the tea interval swims that chaos broke out. Freemo and Spence were in the pool. Pauline ran up to them, loudly shouting "Fire!". Freemo and Spence laughed. "Don't be silly – it's no good trying to sponge us like that!" they smiled.

"No. Really. Fire!"

"Yeah, yeah!"

"THERE'S A FUCKING FIRE!" Pauline almost never swore. The two lads looked at each other, worried now.

They tore off their swimming helmets and ran after Pauline back to the low rise apartment. Sure enough, thick smoke was billowing from the upstairs window. Brian and Brocksie were in the garden, watching, beer in hand.

Spence and Freemo acted quite quickly, considering. They wet their towels, put them over their heads and ran into the downstairs kitchen. Pauline had been cooking beef burgers on the small Calor gas stove. The two lads turned it off and carried the whole thing out into the front garden. The gas canister might have exploded.

Back in they went and managed to make the first floor bedrooms. They threw open the window and carefully dropped the duty frees to Brian and Brocksie below.

Next they threw everything they could find into the still open suitcases and threw these down to soft landings on the hedge below.

The smoke was thick and black by now. The two tried for the top floor bathroom but the combination of sooty smoke and the fact that the janitor had now appeared and begun to poke a hosepipe through the window (this was likely to be an electrical fire) sent them scurrying back.

Having saved the luggage and the duty frees, they decided to quit whilst they were ahead. Emerging back into the front garden, faces blackened by soot, the two lads were greeted by a large crowd of rubber-neckers. Some even burst into a round of applause. Spence

122

and Freemo turned the annoyed janitor's hose off before he electrocuted himself and made sure that someone had called the fire brigade. There was nothing else they could do now.

Hollins and Crowbar had – calm as you like – finished cooking Pauline's burgers and had begun selling them to the crowd of onlookers.

Kelvin stood in the shadows, head in hands. For fucks sake! They hadn't even been here twenty four hours yet. And the apartment they had complained about so vociferously was now burning down! Shit!

The fire brigade arrived in due course and quickly and efficiently put the fire out. Sure enough, it had started because of an electrical heater fault it the third floor bathroom. The apartment had been saved; no one was hurt; all their belongings were safe; the duty frees hadn't boiled away to nothing…. but now the smoke damage had made the apartment uninhabitable.

Deciding that their holiday rep didn't take to kindly to them, the lads got one of the girls to make the call. The rep dropped everything and raced round to survey the damage. Luckily the burgers had sold out and the Fire Brigade were still on site when she arrived. They explained to her that the electrical fire couldn't have been the lads fault. Thank fuck.

As if by magic, one of the better apartments in the high rise block suddenly became available. The six were happily re-housed within the hour. But they had to first agree to the late night trouser washing rule too.

The days leading up to the grudge football match passed happily. The friends had found a great little beach bar where beers and pizzas (proper English pizzas for Brian) were cheap enough. No one in the bar could speak a word of English, though. The only one of their group who had any Italian was Freemo, and that was just Berlitz phrase book Italian (count to ten, say please and thank-you, order beer, order white or red wine, ask where the toilets were, say goodbye). Aided by furiously gesticulating arms and hopefully expressive eye and head movements. Freemo thus earned himself the 'Capitano' nickname from the waitress Lilliano. She simply couldn't believe the amount of beers the lads drank (out of Wellington boot shaped Italian glasses) and needed confirmation of each order. Business had rarely been so good and Capitano and his mates were honoured guests at the establishment every day.

Remarkably, not TOO much else had gone wrong. Yes, there was the Yugoslavian debacle. The lads had booked a day trip across the Adriatic to see Pula. It was to be a very early start (5 a.m.) and so most of them didn't bother going to bed. They assembled at the meeting point on time. Nothing. They waited almost an hour. Nothing. They tried phoning the rep's office. Still nothing. So they found a bar.

It eventually turned out that strong winds had made the sea crossing unsafe and so the trip was cancelled. Someone could've fucking said something!

Relationships with the rep. had now all but broken down completely, especially as there had been further complaints about late night noise. They presented her with a parrots tail feather by way of apology, but it did no good – either for their relationship OR the parrot. Any discussions had to go through the girls. Or Kelvin, who was treated as an honourary girl. The next week's trip to Venice had to be booked that way.

Yes, there as the party on the balcony incident too. Unusually pissed, Crowbar, Freemo and Hollins decided to have a nude party on their balcony. Even Kelvin joined them. It seemed to sort of evolve. Rules were introduced. Eventually the laughter got too loud and Freemo's wife went out there, only to be confronted by three bollock naked blokes - standing on one leg; hopping; comb in their hair; ten thousand lira note rolled and in their left ear. "Fucking hell!". She sighed as she shut the door and went back to bed.

Yes, Kelvin – fed up with the piss taking from the others, had tried to phone his Mum and develop an escape plan to get him home early. It was the start of the "I'm gonna phone my Mummy" chanting. And it only made things worse.

Yes there were the accusations relating to the pissing in the pool from the seventh floor balcony competition, but the author feels it better to gloss over that one.

Yes, there was the unfortunate incident of the mistaken apartment spoof. Hollins, Freemo and Crowbar, after a few beers, got into the lift on the ground floor. They pressed the fifth floor button as well as the seventh floor that they wanted, and then Freemo stood in front of the lights. On arrival at the fifth floor Crowbar got out. The others pressed the door shut button and pretended they hadn't been able to get out in time. They shouted to Crowbar to get the kettle on. Each floor of the block was identical, so Crowbar had no idea he was actually two floors below where he should be. He strode up to what he thought was his apartment door, leant on the buzzer and – when the door opened, walked through to what he thought was his lounge, plonked himself on the sofa and farted loudly. And then realised he was in a German family's apartment. More complaints.

And yes, there were the strange receptions throughout the resorts restaurants as the lads asked for a place to be set for Alan. Alan was a cheap football. With a face drawn on it. He was their inseparable friend – Alan Ball. They bought him drinks and ordered him meals, only to help him out when he couldn't finish them. By the end of the fortnight he had a girlfriend, Peggy. She was a clothes peg. Luckily she was on a diet and didn't drink.

Match day Saturday soon arrived! All week the ninth floorers had been jealously eyeing the beer displayed in the seventh floorers apartment window.

On match day the favourites from the seventh floor laid out their smart yellow and blue matching strips and checked their trainer lacing. The ball was pumped up to the right pressure. The two groups stayed apart for the whole of the day, arranging to meet on the beach at midnight. The ninth floorers got pissed as usual. So did the seventh floorers, confident of their abilities being too much for their opponents.

At midnight, the seventh floorers marched down to the beach in their Spurs tops. They ceremoniously carried the seven pint prize and the match ball. The ninth floorers jeered as they arrived. They had already cleared the pitch of umbrella holders, save for the two at each end which formed the goals. Even the girls came down to watch on the otherwise deserted beach.

The seventh floorers won the toss and kicked off in an atmosphere of real tension. Hollins to Freemo; back to Kelvin. Kelvin pumps the ball up to Freemo, who turns and fizzes a shot which clips the outside of one post before going behind for a goal kick.

Postman Brian recovered the ball, picked it up and threw it fifty yards out to sea! Game over. Nil fucking nil! The sea was too rough for them to get their only ball back and the wind was blowing it further out by the second.

"Best split the beer then!" smirked Brian.

"You can fuck right off you cheating bastard!" retorted Freemo, annoyed.

The seventh floorers marched furiously back to their apartment, letting it be known that they intended to drink all the beer themselves once they got there.

Back in the apartment, the lads calmed down a little. The prize was placed in the middle of the dining table and Freemo attacked it with their opener. Four glasses eagerly awaited filling. Freemo opened the can and filed them all. Each took a simultaneous large gulp. Each spat the beer out simultaneously. The fucking stuff had gone flat! THAT'S what a cold, de-pressurised airplane hold did to beer. Pouring it dolefully down the sink, the seventh floorers decided not to mention this detail to their cheating bastard opponents. Wouldn't give them the satisfaction.

The Venice trip was a success – Freemo learned that Riccione was a seaside resort and very similar to the Italian word for gay boy. Hollins took a handful of water during their gondola trip, and held it to his nose, sniffing. "Hmmm. Canal Number five" he announced.

Most of the lads bought marble chess sets as souvenirs. All of them bought terracotta jugs from Lilliano's bar and left her a large tip. She was overwhelmed.

On the day of departure, Trish reverted to Capitano. She began collecting tickets from the front of the check in queue, only to bump into her husband Crowbar doing the same thing from the back. Crowbar threw his tickets up in the air in surprise as they met in the middle. Trish threw hers up in the air in anger. And things got worse as everyone laughed at the pantomime.

Once checked in, the friends disappeared to departures for an eventless flight back home.

Frankie the Thomson rep. sighed a deep sigh of relief as the last one of them disappeared from view.

Result: 0 – 0 (match abandoned in the 1st minute)

Attendance: 4

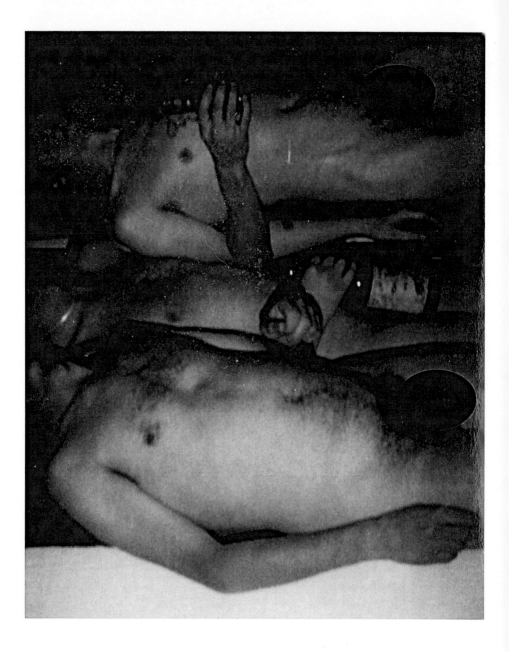

Kelvin, Freemo and Crowbar play up at the balcony party. Hollins, who took this picture, kept it in an envelope marked 'Crowbar's blackmail photo' and extracted the odd pint or two out of him.

Oh and by the way...

~

Cowboy is a big lad. He has worked all his life in the building trade and is definitely a no-nonsense sort of bloke. Very down to earth.

So, when he stopped going to Tottenham games for a few years, most of the lads suspected a new woman. Some thought he might just be losing too much money at cards.

None suspected the truth. He had taken to showing Afghan dogs.

The lads just couldn't imagine Kev trotting gracefully round a show ring, leading a carefully groomed Afghan hound by a pink lead held daintily between thumb and forefinger. But that's how it was.

~

CHAPTER TEN

COVENTRY CITY AT WEMBLEY
F A CUP FINAL WOES
(16/5/1987)

Tottenham had made it to Wembley again! Having already won two F.A. Cup finals this decade (plus a UEFA Cup), Spurs had fought their way past Scunthorpe, Palace, Newcastle, Wimbledon and Watford and were now facing Coventry City in a mid-May final that the lads were sure would go their way. Coventry City were viewed as a much smaller outfit and Clive Allen was banging in goals for fun. Tottenham were red (white?) hot favourites with the bookies.

Despite being a Midlands side, perhaps only thirty or so miles from Worcester, the lads didn't know even ONE Coventry fan in their city. No one to take the piss out of in the build up to the game.

Freemo was living in Yorkshire now and doing well at work – he had been promoted to senior management at Grattan / Next (the two companies had merged). The M.D., David Jones, yet again came up trumps for him and two tickets just appeared on his desk one morning. Really good seats on the half way line. Again Freemo vowed unswerving loyalty.

But for this game he needed an extra ticket for his brother Nigel. And it was proving hard to come by.

By 1987, Freemo had left his wife and was seeing a colleague from work – also a Julie (he reckoned it was a good idea in case he talked in his sleep to go out with girls who had the same name!). Julie Two worked in the buying department for the main Grattan Catalogue, and catalogue buyers are well treated when it comes to samples and perks.

One of her colleagues was Pat Wall – a staunch (and often militant) socialist who was an ally of Derek Hatton. Pat was a big Everton fan and, despite their clashing political views, Freemo liked him. They once went to an Everton – Spurs game together at Goodison and had a great day out. Not even a hint of a political discussion all day.

Pat worked on buying household goods and hardware and one of his suppliers, Swann, had offered him a V.I.P. place at the cup final. Pat didn't fancy it and, knowing that Freemo needed a ticket, offered it to him via Julie. The only condition was that Freemo himself used it as it involved a pre-match drinks reception, meeting a couple of ex-players and high tea afterwards. All with a complimentary bar.

Freemo gratefully snapped his hand off for it. He agreed with Julie that she and Freemo jnr. would use the pair of half way line seats, whilst he endured the corporate hospitality. Julie wasn't best pleased – jnr. could be a bit of a handful when he'd had a drink and she really wanted to watch the match with her partner – but she agreed.

The Worcester lads had mostly managed to get tickets from the usual sources – a few from Tottenham, some from the local F.A., some from personal contacts. But almost everyone had a ticket.

Travel arrangements were a bit disjointed and so, when Freemo rang Smiffy to find out what was happening – and found out nothing had been organised – he suggested that he drove his company car down to Wembley via Worcester. He had to pick up his brother anyhow and so it was all quickly agreed.

Freemo checked with Pat and discovered that the dress code for his corporate day was lounge suit and tie. Bollocks. He dug out a Spurs tie and bought a huge navy and white Tottenham rosette, intent on showing the prawn sandwich brigade that he was a partisan Spurs fan…. and not just for the day. Most of those there would be neutrals who chose one team or the other for the day, most probably rooting for the Coventry underdogs. They probably wouldn't have ever been to a game in their life. Most likely Man.Utd. or Chelsea 'fans'.

Freemo and Julie decided to travel down to Worcester after work on the Friday night, ready for an early start the next day and so the two set out at around five, negotiated the M62 across the Pennines, skirted Manchester and then turned south onto the M6.

Freemo had got into the habit of a pub stop near where the M6 joined the M5 and so, a couple of hours after setting out, the Volvo turned off the motorway and left onto the Cannock road.

About a mile along there, on the left, was a Banks's pub. Freemo and Julie entered the scruffy establishment and inspected the height of the landlord. Freemo had this theory. The guy had the smelliest feet either of them had ever had the misfortune to catch a whiff of. And he wore the same scruffy pair of slippers whatever the weather outside. Tartan fuckers. Filthy. With sticky black residue all over them. Clearly his feet were rotting away and he viewed these as orthopaedic footwear. And each time he went in the pub, Freemo checked the bloke's height to see if any more of his feet had disintegrated. From the smell, it seemed they must have.

They quickly ordered a pint and a martini and retired to the furthest away corner of the pub. Old 'slippers' wasn't having them escape that easily – he very soon came over and started fussing around their table, wiping ashtrays and tables down as he went.

Freemo nicked a paper and went to the bogs until he'd finished polluting their table. Julie brassed it out. When Freemo returned after about ten minutes she was almost green, but 'slippers' had given up and gone back behind the bar.

So Freemo ordered more drinks and they safely drank them before resuming their journey to Worcester.

After a quick beer with bruv. and a phone call to Smiffy to confirm an eight o'clock pick up, Freemo and Julie turned in for the night at a city centre hotel. There wouldn't be time for breakfast with such an early start, but Freemo figured that they could grab something at Sainsbury's as they filled up with beers.

All too soon it was tomorrow, and the reluctant pair showered and began the round of pick ups. Nige was last as he lived nearest to the supermarket.

There were only four in the car today and so there was plenty of room. The Sainsbury's stop was rushed and – after a quick hi to Mrs. Buzz. on the checkout – the carload set out for Wembley.

The journey down was pretty uneventful really. Drinking and chatter. The occasional fart. The occasional frown. The rustle of newspapers and the reading out loud of previews of the match. Then the problem pages.

In a couple of hours the friends were parked up in that fucking NCP that everyone hated. Smiffy didn't miss the opportunity to have a pop at Freemo. "You moan like fuck when I park here!" he remarked, pointedly. "Ah, but you'll have to wait around after the game anyhow" Freemo responded. "I've got to go and take tea with the corporates, remember?".

This year the fan numbers were more equal. Yes, Spurs supporters had got hold of slightly more tickets than Coventry (because they were better positioned to get 'neutrals' seats, being based in London). But Coventry had never won the F.A. Cup and their fans were really up for their big day out. They didn't get many.

And so the car park of 'The Torch' was more even this year – only just over half were Spurs. And the Coventry contingent seemed to have lashed out more on flags. The banter was good natured enough. Each set of fans sang their songs, but the singing wasn't directed at their opponents. Everyone seemed to be having a good, beery day out. It was as Wembley days should be.

Freemo kissed Julie and wagged a finger at Freemo jnr. for one last time. "Remember that my boss got you that fucking ticket" he warned. "And that any trouble or pissed up behaviour will come back directly on me. So fucking behave yourself, mate, eh?". Nige. half re-assured him. "Give him a clip round the ear if he plays up!" Freemo said to Julie, winking as he walked off to find the corporate entrance. It was too early for the march up Wembley Way. He missed that.

He donned his jacket, fastened his top shirt button and straightened his tie as he approached the hospitality area. Showing his ticket to the doorman, Freemo was waved into the large lounge where perhaps forty or fifty privileged individuals, glasses in hand, chatted politely about the weather. Or work. Or Swann fucking kettles. Anything but football it seemed!

But Freemo was used to these sort of cocktail party atmospheres. Lots of falseness. It was something you just had to endure as part of business etiquette. Especially if the fuckers gave you a Spurs cup final ticket and free booze too!

137

So he joined in the frivolous chatter with people he didn't know – and if he did know he would probably not have liked. Especially the one who, on seeing his rosette, had to own up to actually being a Manchester United fan. Wonderful flowing football, don't you know. Wanker.

Brendan Batson was one of the ex-footballers helping with the hosting. Freemo remembered that he used to be a Goon early in his career and studiously avoided shaking hands with him.

A sweep was started. Each participant drew a name out of the hat – eleven Spurs players plus two subs, eleven Coventry players plus two subs and one ticket for 'no goals' – twenty seven tickets in all. They all paid two quid and the one who pulled the first goal scorer took the kitty.

Freemo was pleased when he drew Clive Allen. A good chance of making a bob or two there! He ate a little from the buffet lunch and drank as much as he politely could. He took his seat outside as early as he could to try to get some big match atmosphere.

Inside the arena, the same pattern as in the pub car park emerged. There were slightly more Spurs fans, but Coventry had more flags and banners. This was Tottenham's sixth Wembley final in six years and the fans had got a bit lazy, it seemed. Coventry's fans sang their hearts out. Spurs fans, relaxed, sang occasionally.

Cup final hymns sung and the national anthem belted out from all around the stadium, the game kicked off bang on three o'clock.

Spurs started well. Chris Waddle created Tottenham's opening goal by showing the ball to Greg Downs, dragging it away from him and then centring towards the near post. Clive Allen easily scored with a close-range header. Yahoo! And Freemo had won over fifty quid too!

As always seemed the case with Spurs, they sat back after scoring. Within seven minutes Coventry had levelled. Houchen's flick caused chaos in the Spurs defence and as they left the ball for goalkeeper Clemence, Dave Bennett – their only player with Cup Final experience (for Manchester City in 1981) – toe poked it into the net.

City then had a real let-off after a series of stupid mistakes on the half hour.

Trevor Peake's under-hit a back-pass didn't reach the penalty-area and their keeper, Ogrizovic, tried to dribble the ball out of away.

His attempted left-footed clearance was blocked by Hoddle who then tried to chip the ball into the empty goal but only managed to find Peake trying to make up for his error by running back to cover.

But Peake merely compounded his earlier error by inexplicably passing the ball to Tottenham's prolific Clive Allen. Luckily for City forty nine goal Allen shot tamely into the side netting.

Spurs did take the lead again on forty minutes when Ogrizovic crazily came out to collect a Hoddle free-kick from the right. Everyone could see he had no hope of getting there. The ball fell between Brian Kilcline and Gary Mabbutt and as both players stuck out a leg. Mabs got there first and turned it into the net.

In the second half, Tottenham turned up the heat and were threatening to take total control. But it was Coventry who scored next. Bennett broke away down the right wing and crossed for Houchen to dive full length and head a brilliant goal. The Tottenham fans were stunned, fully expecting to score a third and put the game to bed.

Glenn Hoddle had been subdued for most of his farewell performance before moving to Monaco and the match moved into extra time.

At the end of a surging run down the right, Coventry's Lloyd McGrath hit over a hopeful cross-cum-shot which took a wicked deflection off Mabbutt's outstretched leg and looped over the Ray Clemence's head into the net. Try as they might, Spurs couldn't fashion an equaliser.

Freemo trudged back to the hospitality area, thoroughly pissed off. Julie, Nige and Smiffy went back to wait at the car.

Freemo couldn't suppress a scowl as he was presented with his fifty four quid and the assembled Man Utd fans politely applauded. Fuck 'em.

As soon as was possible, he made his excuses and returned to the car park. Julie and Freemo jnr. were in the car, miserable. Smiffy was looking out over the rail of the car parks top deck. Freemo joined him. No-one said a word. Nige appeared and thrust a can into his hand. Still no-one spoke – they were all close to tears.

Eventually the ice was broken by an unlikely scene below. An open top bus passed. In the middle of the top deck was a huge barrel of beer. All the occupants were dressed in full cockerel suits. And as the bus passed, the pissed up crowd burst into a rendition of "E-Ay-Adio, we lost the cup!". The lads began to laugh. And talk. And drive.

They managed to get away from the car park. Freemo fancied a proper beer in a proper pub, and so – once the North Circular was largely cleared, they pulled into a large pub next to the Rolls Royce garage. No one had ever seemed to know its name.

The pub was one of those long thin ones. Bar at the front, lounge at the back. The friends plonked themselves in the first available seat and ordered their drinks, Freemo had long since discarded his suit and tie.

They settled quietly into their beers. The power of speech began to return, albeit slowly. Turns out Freemo jnr. disgraced himself. He got thoroughly pissed and when he and Julie got to their very-nice-thank-you seats, proceeded to stand on his, singing at the top of his voice and offering to fight any Coventry fans who were prepared to listen. Fortunately his fighting ability was severely curtailed as – pissed as he was – his seat tipped up, his legs fell through and he was trapped between the seat and the seat back. No one, including Julie, felt to inclined to help him out until he had calmed down a bit. Thanks junior.

Freemo bollocked his younger brother for acting like a prat and Nige took it shamefacedly enough. But somehow they both knew it would be just the same next time. Oh well.

They all lapsed back into a silence only broken by occasional jerky attempts at chatter. Freemo bought a few rounds out of his winnings. When they couldn't be bothered to talk, they just read their cup final programmes for something to do. Loads more adverts than usual, it seemed.

After a few rounds, Jimmy announced that he had better call Lesley who for some unimaginable reason he had arranged to meet in Worcester for a drink that evening. Fucking Hell! It was ten to eight already.

There was a payphone in their part of the bar and Smiffy made his way to it. "What shall I tell her Freemo", he asked the driver.

"Tell her there was extra time" retorted Freemo. Smiffy turned away, dialled and dropped numerous coins into the phone.

"Hello darling. Me here" he began lamely.

The lads only heard one end of the conversation, but it went something like this:-

"Yes, I know. Crap today darling" (Lesley must've been sympathising).

"How was your day?" (Smiffy was obviously creeping before breaking the bad news).

"Not sure exactly dear. There was extra time you see." (Lesley had clearly asked the million dollar question).

"Yes, I realise you watched it and that was a while ago now. Hang on, I'll ask Freemo, darling". (Lesley had seen through his first ploy and Smiffy was passing the buck onto Freemo).

Putting his hand over the phone, he shouted across the room to Freemo. "Lesley would like to know if I'll be home in time to take her out as promised" he said hopefully. His hand had partly covered the phone so she could hear it wasn't his fault. Freemo didn't give a toss.

"Tell her no fucking chance" he shouted loudly. After all, he'd only just begun having a proper drink!

Smiffy turned his back and continued, weakly "Malcolm says it's very unlikely darling. Sorry, but I am at everyone else's mercy here".

141

Lesley hung up on him. So they stayed late and drank lots more beer. Smiffy was sick in the car on the way home. It took Freemo a week to find out that the reason he couldn't wipe it off was that it was on the INSIDE of the rear window!

The day that ruined a good Monty Python sketch was over. Thank fuck. The fact that this Cup final is widely regarded as one of the classics was of no consolation whatsoever.

Result : Coventry City 3 – 2 Tottenham Hotspur (Clive Allen, Mabbutt)

Attendance ; 98,000

Oh and by the way...

~

Mick (aka Crowbar) tired of his job at Berrows and took redundancy. He had met a new mate – an eccentric character, also called Mick – and they spent a lot of time together. To give you some idea, eccentric Mick was an ex-monk who had been thrown out of numerous council houses for keeping chickens and goats in the garden. Most of the lads were wary of him. Stick just hated him full stop.

In any case, the two decided to go into business together. For some reason, they decided on a mobile butchers business – Mick Mick Meats. The idea was to travel round council estates where there were few butchers and sell well priced cuts of meat from pub car parks.

They bought and converted an old ice cream van. It was ideal as it was refrigerated, spacious and had a selling hatch. The van was resprayed and sign-written. The ice cream chimes were changed to a mooing cow.

Initially, the business went well. They expanded into selling salads to picnickers and burgers to by-passers and the money was coming in nicely.

It all started to go tits up when Crowbar lost his licence through drinking and driving. At that point they bought a butcher's shop which Crowbar ran whilst Mick the monk did the van round.

Crowbar knew fuck all about butchery. The shop was raided by animal rights campaigners. Mick the monk spent all day in the Crown and Anchor instead of selling.

Ah well, nice try lads.

~

CHAPTER ELEVEN

FREEMO'S SECOND WEDDING
HOLLINS CREATES HAVOC
(1/5/1989)

Freemo had been misbehaving. Again. Through work he had met a girl, also named Julie and they had secretly started seeing each other. Freemo was still married and Julie was living with a guy. Things came to a head when her boyfriend discovered what was going on, went berserk with a kitchen knife and got on the phone to Freemo in the middle of the night. Freemo had no option but to wake his wife, admit what was going on and get over to try to sort out the mess at the other end. It was the morning of April 1st and initially, his wife didn't believe him.

Having been thrown together in this way, Freemo had felt rushed along in the early days.... but Julie needed looking after and he felt he must protect her. When things became less pressurised and they were still together, he realised that they had something good going on.

The couple decided to get married. A Church wedding might be a bit of a problem in the circumstances, so they began investigating weddings abroad. Anyone who has ever done this will soon realise that to marry in an English speaking country makes quite a lot of sense – things are easier to organise and the legal documents don't need translation (at about a hundred quid a page). It had to be somewhere warm too.

Brochures were scoured and discarded – too costly, too cold, too noisy, too many kids, too small to do weddings. But after a while they had narrowed things down and eventually settled on a hotel in Ocho Rios in Jamaica.

Freemo waited until Spurs were knocked out of the Cup before agreeing to an early May date. You usually have to be in the country for a week before you can marry and eventually they settled on 1st May. Freemo reckoned he'd always get a day off for his anniversary. There was a bit of a hurdle to overcome in telling Julie's Mum that it was just going to be the two of them, but that was what they had decided and so they broke the news to a mixed reaction. Julie's Mum was delighted that they were to get married, but extremely pissed off that she wasn't invited. And she told the couple so, saying they were being selfish.

Freemo, though, had always had a plan. Hollins had been best man (at least one of two best men) at Freemo's first wedding and was now living in the U.S. Not too far away, Freemo reckoned, dismissing the facts. Because Hollins was going to be invited, and because Julie's Mum had lost her youngest son in a tragic coach accident, he secretly hatched a plan to fly Julie's Mum out for a week so she could be there at the wedding.

Lots of secret conversations took place. Julie's brother and sister-in-law were all brought in on the secret. Julie thought Freemo was planning something with Hollins, but didn't suspect the truth. Gradually, it seemed, the whole world except Julie knew the big secret.

Hollins had agreed to be best man and was looking forward to meeting up with his mate again in the sunshine. He was planning to arrive a few days after Freemo and stay until after the wedding.

Julie and Freemo booked the holiday / wedding / honeymoon package and found that, on the dates in question, if they booked two weeks they got a third week free. Result!

Independently Freemo spent a lot of time and trouble booking a seven night holiday for Julie's Mum. Even bought her a bottle of champagne for the flight over. She was thrilled.

Hollins phoned to say that he was having 'one or two problems' which meant he was a bit skint. So he would be booking into a cheap hotel down the road a few miles. He'd explain when they met up. Hmmm.

All the usual wedding preamble took place – Julie's Mum even went shopping for a dress with her daughter and kept up the pretence of moaning about not being invited.

All their friends had sent them cards for the big day and before they knew it, it was late April and they set out from their Amersham home for the airport. There was still a chill in the air as they arrived, parked up and flew off to the sun.

The hotel they had booked – The Shaw Park Beach - was nice enough. The rooms were a bit small though. And the en-suites could have done with a re-grout. Freemo always took a copy of the brochure they had booked from away with him – that way he could check that they were getting everything that had been advertised. He fished it out and scoured the small print as Julie unpacked, discovering that they were entitled to upgrade to the best available room on arrival. They hadn't received the fruit and flowers in the room which their wedding also entitled them to, so he made a mental note to try to sort things out the next day. Too tired now after that long, alcohol filled flight.

So after a couple of Yellow Birds and the odd Bloody Mary, they turned it in and listened to the chirruping crickets as they fell asleep. As usual when you travel long haul east to west, they awoke very early the next morning. Too early for breakfast – their heads were still on English time. They fiddled with the T.V. to find out what channels were available. They got up, showered and finished unpacking. And eventually it got light.

The wedding was set for late morning on Monday 1st May. Julie's Mum was due to arrive during the afternoon of the day before, with the plan being for her to emerge from behind something as the couple married. Hollins was due to arrive on the Thursday before the big day, so they had a few days to themselves, which they happily filled by drinking cocktails, sunbathing and swimming. Plus the odd meeting with officialdom to organise wedding related things like cakes, buttonholes, bouquets and so on. Freemo had to sneak back later and order an extra buttonhole for Julie's Mum.

Having met a Canadian bloke who had been upgraded to a suite on the second night, Freemo arranged to have a look at it the next day.

149

Palatial! Two double bedrooms, each with two queen sized beds. Two bathrooms. Huge lounge. Terrace right down by the beach. Freemo asked the Canadian, as he wasn't getting married, how he got the upgrade and the Canadian – stoned – admitted that the manager must've just liked him.

Freemo booked an appointment with the hotel manager to show him the 'best available room' wedding offer and, after a bit of to-ing and fro-ing, he and Julie were upgraded to a similar deluxe oceanfront suite. With fruit and flowers. And a complimentary bottle of Tia Maria which was replaced with a full one each morning! Happy days.

Hollins arrived and met the couple by the pool. He was a day late and had arrived in Jamaica with one straw hat (with scarf attached), one set of clothes (the ones he was wearing), 16 cans of Heineken lager and a credit card stolen from his wife. That was the problem he hadn't explained – he had split with his American wife Jennie and she was seeing someone else. So, being skint, he'd nicked her credit card and come anyhow.

Hollins had booked into a cheap hotel in Ocho Rios itself – about two miles away. He had only paid one night's deposit and was going to have to settle the balance on the dodgy card. Freemo looked at Julie. Julie looked at Freemo. After all, they did have a spare room and a spare bathroom. She sighed, knowing how strong the bond was between the two. And that's how Hollins came to be slinging his bag over the wall by the hotel's back gate late that night. Freemo caught it and took it to the room. It was easy really – Pete then just walked in through the main entrance, had a few beers with the wedding couple, and then didn't leave again. A start like that maybe told Julie something, Freemo reckoned in later years.

On Hollins' first morning he skipped breakfast, deciding it was best not to be seen. Instead he stayed in the room and tried to tune in Freemo's short wave radio to pick up the football scores. Because of the time difference, kick off was at 10 a.m. Jamaican time.

Freemo and Julie re-appeared with Mick and Majella, friends and fellow Spurs fans from Jersey who they met on the beach. By now Hollins had given up on inside reception and was busy balancing on a table, trying his best to attach a crocodile clip aerial booster to the spiral metal fire escape to the side of the apartment. With some joy too – through the crackling they could pick up the occasional English voice. Tottenham were away to Millwall that day and were expected to win.

They cracked open a beer each to kick off the football party and then took turns to try to make sense of the crackling. Someone upstairs was on their side that day as the results came in. "Millwall nil, crackleham five" they clearly heard! That was the signal for the party to kick off properly. Mick rescued a bottle of duty free blue vodka from his room. They sent Dixie, the windsurfing shack bloke, off to get a case of Red Stripe too. Then there was the Tia Maria. Freemo didn't make dinner that day. Mick ribbed him about it next day and Freemo only discovered about a week later that Mick hadn't made it either. Bastard!

Freemo had told Hollins to keep a low profile and paid for his dinner each night. It all went pretty smoothly. Initially. Then the drinking began to get heavier.

The next two nights entertainment were chaotic! First Pete nearly got into a fight over the crab racing. The idea was that six crabs, each with a different coloured spot of paint on their shell, was put into a clear bucket and displayed. The 'race goers' bet on a lively looking one and – when it was time – the crab bucket was upturned in the centre of a painted circle. First crab to leave the circle was the winner. Freemo and Hollins would never bet on the red crab, but it was well supported…. and about to win. Until, that is, Pete stamped his foot very hard, very close to the poor thing. It did the crab equivalent of put its claws over its eyes and stopped dead. Pete's crab stormed past and won. Pete overdid the celebrations and the irate Canadian red crab backers became violent.

The following night was no better. Mick, Majella, Julie and Freemo were enjoying the reggae band but couldn't believe their ears as the singer suddenly went wildly out of tune. They looked round and – to Freemo's horror – Hollins had pushed the singer off the stage and was belting out a very pissed version of 'No Woman No Cry!'. And, even though it was probably the most awful rendition they had ever heard, the audience loved it. Stood on their seats and cheered him on, they did. So what did Petey boy do? Forgot the words and fell over! Freemo was horrified. And in between episodes, he had formed a friendship with the entertainments manageress. A close friendship shall we say. So much for the low profile, 'Ol!. Freemo was sure that was the only thing that saved him from being outed as a stowaway. But for one reason or another she didn't let out his secret to her hotel management colleagues.

By now, of course, the party were famous (infamous?) among the other hotel guests. All of them knew the big wedding secret too. Freemo went to great lengths to make sure no-one spoiled the surprise.

Sunday arrived – the day before the wedding. Suit and dresses had been laundered to get the travel creases out. Mick and Majella offered to take the photos as a wedding present. After one last check with their wedding co-ordinator, both Freemo and Julie were happy that everything was properly in hand and nothing more needed to be done, so they relaxed for the rest of the day. Outwardly, that is. Freemo was anxious that when Julie's mum arrived at about nine that evening, she was kept away from the bride to be. And he charged his best man with meeting her, organising food (she probably wouldn't have eaten) and letting her know about the arrangements for the next day.

By mid afternoon, Julie tired of the sun and went back to the air conditioning to shower and get ready for dinner. Freemo and Hollins were left chatting to two girls from Blackpool. And flirting a bit.

Dinner came and went. Freemo suggested an early night and Julie agreed. Big day ahead. Hollins stayed at the bar, ready to perform his secret duties.

The bridal couple showered and bedded down, excited about the day to come. The cocktails helped them sleep. At least one of them. Freemo mock snored to re-assure his partner and soon she was away with the fairies. He waited half an hour, not daring to move, and then checked on his partner. Mouth wide open, flat on her back. In any other circumstances....

So he slipped as quietly as he could from the bed, tip-toed to the door and crept out into the living room, slowly closing the door behind him. Freemo had left flip-flops, shorts and a shirt there and he quickly pulled them on. Julie's Mum should have arrived by now and he wanted to say a quick hello. Silently opening the bedroom door, he slid out into the Caribbean night and turned right to the room he knew Julie's mum was being housed in.

He hurried along the sand and knocked at the door of her room, which Hollins duly opened. Fair play to him – he had done everything he should and was getting on famously with Julie's mum. She had been rushed through check in; had eaten a sandwich; knew the wedding arrangements. Most unlike Pete! Freemo gave her a hug and asked if she needed anything else. When she said she didn't, he took her to see where the wedding would be the next day and they agreed on a good hiding place behind a palm tree. That done, Freemo took his leave and headed back to the apartment. He walked back along the beach, but as he took his flip flops off to sneak back in, he noticed something was wrong. The apartment lights were on. All of them.

Taking the bull by the horns, he walked in through the sliding doors to find Julie watching T.V. from one of the lounge chairs.

"Where the bloody hell have you been sneaking off to?" she glared.

"I couldn't sleep and so I went for a bit of air on the beach" lied Freemo. It would be such a shame to spoil the surprise at this stage. But Julie seemed intent on just that.

"Don't lie to me" she shouted. "I'm not stupid you know. You've been with that Pete Holland, haven't you?. You've been off with those two girls from Blackpool I saw you with earlier!".

Freemo was hugely annoyed, but daren't show it. She was being unreasonable and unfair…. and if only she knew the truth. Freemo tried to calm things down, but in the end let her rage on and went to bed. Angry.

The next day brought an awkward silence at breakfast and re-assurances from Freemo that he and Pete hadn't been bonking the

Lancastrians by way of a stag party. For the sake of the wedding, Freemo ate humble pie, apologised and things were smoothed over. He hated apologising, especially when he was in the right. Some start to the marriage he thought, anxiously and secretly.

The wedding couple showered and dressed. Pete had borrowed one of Freemo's white shirts for the occasion – he hadn't brought a shirt. The buttonholes arrived. All except Julie's Mum's thank God! In his white shirt and sporting a matching buttonhole, Hollins had begun to scrub up half decently. He vacated the apartment as the couple dressed. And he vowed to spend their wedding night on the beach. One potentially awkward situation handled then.

The wedding co-ordinator came to fetch them five minutes before the eleven o'clock wedding and they held hands as they walked the path to the wedding arch. Half way there, though, the co-ordinator took a phone call – all was not ready and they had to return to the room.

After a five minute delay, filled with a swift Tia Maria and a squirt of Gold Spot, they set off again on their walk. It was a breezy Caribbean morning. As they turned the corner which revealed the all important palm tree, out stepped Julie's Mum. Probably smiling. A huge gust of wind blew her hat over her face at exactly the wrong moment.

It took a while to sink in. And then there were tears. From Julie. From her Mum. From the thirty or forty hotel staff and guests who had gathered to see this wonderful surprise. And from Freemo. Soft bastard.

Excitement over, the couple married, ate cake, drank wine and listened to the resident hotel band sing some song about a phallic big bamboo. Hollins discreetly disappeared. The party – it now firmly included Mick and Majella with whom the three had become firm friends – met for dinner in the open air later that evening, by which time Hollins had had a few. Between each course, he insisted on beginning a best man speech. The party laughed each time he scraped back his chair and began "Unaccustomed as I am….". But each time they barracked him and he sat back down. This was the longest of short best man's speeches. It eventually took him two days to deliver it all.

In the days that followed, Freemo had some long heart to hearts with 'Ol. His break up had really affected him a lot deeper than he was ready to admit. The drinking, always legendary, was now becoming a problem. It meant he was putting on weight, so he made himself sick after each meal. Freemo remarked "Fucking hell Pete, why tell me now? I could've saved a fortune on your dinners!". He didn't really understand, but he did make Pete promise not to do it on this holiday, at least. And as far as he knew, Pete kept that promise.

After her week, Julie's Mum was waved off. Seven days isn't a long time for a long haul holiday and she wanted longer. But she understood that it wouldn't be right to have Mum along for ALL of the honeymoon.

And then it was time for Pete to leave. Due to finances, he had travelled across from Texas to Miami on a Greyhound bus, then hopped on a one hour flight from there. The bus journey had taken three days. Freemo appreciated the effort but he was worried about the journey back. Yes, Pete had his return tickets, but he had no money whatsoever. Freemo had made him get rid of the stolen credit card.

Normal Rob, one of Freemo's Worcester mates, had generously given the couple an unsigned U.S. $50 travellers cheque as a wedding present. So Freemo gave it to Pete so that he could at least eat on the way home. Most of it went on beer.

FOOTNOTE: The scorers in the victory against Millwall were Stewart (who got a hat-trick), Walsh and Samways. The crowd was 16,551. The fighting in the area apparently went on well into the evening.

Oh and by the way...

~

Freemo had an almost new Ford Granada – a company car. He drove it down to Leicester early on the Saturday morning of the match. Arriving about opening time, he parked it in a wide road near to the ground and close to his first destination – The Turnstile pub.

Freemo and his wife Julie went into the pub and joined the few other Tottenham fans already there. He took the drinking steadily as the numbers grew and then went off to the match.

On returning, he was confused. Sure that he was in the right street, he couldn't find his car. Moreover, the street was lined with 'No Parking' cones.

Sensible Keith happened along and when Freemo explained his confusion, asked "Wasn't a Grey Granada was it Malc?". "Yes, why?" replied Freemo. "Well I don't know how to tell you this but the Police towed it away about one o'clock" Keith said.

Fucking Hell!

Freemo dialled 999 and shouted at everyone who came on the line. He discovered that his car had, indeed, been towed away. The road he had chosen to park in was apparently a safety route for the emergency services to have access to the stadium.

But they only put the cones out at fucking midday and he had parked there before eleven! Because of this, he was told there would be no charge for reclaiming the vehicle (why do Police always proceed down the street, not walk? Why do they always talk about vehicles, not cars or vans? Wankers!).

Freemo was partly placated, until he discovered that the 'vehicle compound' was three fucking miles away! Not having a taxi number or a clue what bus to get, he and Julie trudged off and, after over an hour, found the Police station they had been told to report to.

Breath smelling strongly of Polo mints, Freemo strode indignantly up to the counter and was told to wait in line. He lost it

"Never mind wait in line! Give me my fucking car back you fucking wankers!" he shouted.

But when a couple of the desk Sergeant's colleagues quickly appeared and threatened to nick him, he soon calmed down. Not worth it. To their credit they apologised and brought the car round to the front entrance within minutes

Date: Sat 13th April 1985

Result : Leicester City. 1 – 2 Tottenham Hotspur (Hoddle, Falco)

Attendance ; 15,609

~

CHAPTER TWELVE

BORO AWAY
THE EMPIRE STRIKES BACK
(29/1/89)

THE BARCLAYS LEAGUE DIVISION ONE
SATURDAY 21st JANUARY 1989
MIDDLESBROUGH v. TOTTENHAM HOTSPUR
KICK OFF - 3.00 pm

HERITAGE
Hampers
OFFICIAL SHIRT
SPONSORS
1988/89

TODAY'S
MATCH SPONSORS
JOSHUA TETLEY
NORTH EAST

OFFICIAL
PROGRAMME
£1.00

MIDDLESBROUGH

It was Richie Rich who made the suggestion – he and Freemo were good friends. They played golf over at Iver most Sundays – two rounds of nine holes, then a few pints of Guinness, then back to one or other of their houses for Sunday lunch. Richie was an ex soldier – well actually he was nicked at the Anderlecht home game and was found to have gone AWOL. He spent a few weeks in the glasshouse in Colchester after that. But he was a good lad – very game and a nice bloke too. He was married to Suzanne and they had a young son. Suzanne came from Newcastle where her Mum and Gran still lived. Nice girl.

Richie's suggestion was that, as Spurs were due to play Middlesbrough in a few weeks, the two couples went and stopped with Su's Mum, had a night out with her and then stopped off to the game on the Saturday whilst the girls did a shopping tour of duty. Suzanne's Mum (and Gran for that matter) were very young looking for their respective ages – they even looked alike. You had to count the rings to tell them apart. The idea sounded good to Freemo, so after a few more pints they went back to Richie's place. His turn this week.

They were greeted by that wonderful 'Sunday lunch is almost ready' smell. They cracked a couple of cans and sat down to negotiations over the succulent roast lamb with all the trimmings.

Richie got bravest first. He began with a surprising amount of subtlety for him.

"We haven't seen your Mum for ages" he threw in, smiling a lazy smile.

"What do you normally do, go up and stop weekends?" supported Freemo.

Silence.

Suzanne broke into a big smile. "You must think I'm daft Rick" she said. "I KNOW Spurs are playing in the North East in three weeks. I've already spoken to Mum and it's all fixed. "So you're coming too, Freemo?" she asked, raising one blonde eyebrow.

"ER... um... well, I'd have to ask Julie first. What do you think?". He tried to recover.

Julie shrugged. "Why not?" she said. "Can I come to the game too?".

Freemo was on the ropes. Suzanne saw it and came to his rescue. "Well, there's fabulous shopping in Gateshead. Why don't we do a girlie afternoon and spend a bit of their money?".

Julie looked uncertain, but agreed to keep the peace.

"Well if you're SURE darling". Freemo pushed his luck and got a mildly suppressed glare for his trouble.

Richie and Freemo dropped the subject as soon as they possibly could. Quit while you're ahead! The conversation switched via Tottenham's performance the day before, through the hard fought draw at golf that morning and on to something that grabbed the girls' interest – what holiday plans each couple had for that year. Freemo felt a bit awkward. He was MD of a company just off Baker Street in central London and was earning big money. Richie and Su didn't earn as much and their holidays were – necessarily – a little more modest. Freemo always tried hard not to appear flash. When Suzanne sighed, he pointed out that her holiday would be much more fun for their young son. How many kids of that age would holiday in Goa, for Christ's sake? Richie and Suzanne were good, proud people – hugely hospitable; always buying rounds – even when it wasn't their turn. A big change from the shallow and false people Freemo had to work with most of the time. He liked and respected these two a great deal.

More beers. On to happy chatter about nothing very much over dessert. A game of sweary Scrabble. Sort out the washing up. And then it was time for them to split up and get ready for the next day's work. Freemo had to catch a Chiltern line just after eight o'clock, so it wasn't too bad. A twenty five minute trip into Marylebone and then an eight minute walk would make sure he was in work enthusiastically early to set the right example. Most days. Richie had to get up much earlier. He was a self employed white-van-man who got his work from a company based at Heathrow airport. The occasional 'extra stock' which came his way helped to boost his income. It seemed incredible to Freemo just what 'got lost' at Heathrow. A whole rack of sheepskin coats and three air-conditioning units for example. Or so rumour had it.

And so the couples exchanged goodbye hugs and prepared to settle back into their weekday rituals again.

On the Monday, Freemo spent the first half hour researching train times, behind a firmly closed office door and armed with the cup of strong black coffee which propelled him back into humanity each morning.

He belled Richie. Richie passed it on to Stuart – an occasional Sunday golfing partner who had relatives (and a place to stay) in Sunderland. He was up for it too.

Freemo managed to sort the match tickets. Middlesbrough was a long way to travel, but as usual Tottenham completely sold out their allocation. Freemo had two season tickets though, and had no problem blagging a spare voucher for Stuey. He didn't mention that Stuart's ticket came from him, just in case Julie kicked off again. No sense in inviting trouble.

The friends all met in the buffet bar on Kings Cross station at around five o'clock on the Friday afternoon. They loaded up with beers and boarded the Newcastle train, walking most of the way through it in an attempt to find two lots of four seats with central tables. After negotiating the first class section, then the buffet car, they struck lucky. Two sat on one side of the aisle; three on the other. They quickly spread out and shared the booze over the two adjacent tables. That should put others off from sitting next to these obvious louts. On one occasion, much to the girls' disgust, Stuart managed to fart aggressively when a middle aged couple began eyeing the seats. The other lads, pretending to be disgusted, silently applauded.

The journey passed quickly and happily until Stu had to get off for his connection to Sunderland – he was staying there with relatives on his Dad's side of the family. They all shook hands and arranged to meet on Middlesbrough station at ten the next morning. The train sped on the short distance to Newcastle and the remaining four poured themselves off the train onto the platform. Their tables resembled a rubbish dump, complete with rows of empty cans, wine bottles, dog-eared papers and food wrappers.

After the usual fumble for train tickets they caught a cab from the rank outside to Suzanne's Mum's house – a modern semi detached in a nice suburb of the city. Reassured that they had eaten (because she had too), Mrs. Su relaxed and offered the lads a bottle of Newcie brown. After a polite hour, Richie suggested the pub. Only Freemo wanted it, and the two somehow managed to get a pass out for an hour or two.

The pub Richie had in mind was only a few hundred yards away. He often escaped there to avoid boring family conversations and old photo albums. It was one of those distinctly Northern pubs. Manly with only the occasional token woman. Full of brown ale drinkers playing dominoes. But an escape, all the same, from the conversation involving fucking shopping plans. There wasn't too much time before closing and so the pair knocked a few quickies back. With chasers. As they weren't locals, there was 'nay chance' of a lock in, so they stumbled the short distance home not much after eleven. Freemo wanted to get a cab. They were a bit pissed.

Soon to bed, the alarm – set for 7:30 – seemed to go off as soon as their swirling heads touched their pillows. Fuck it! The alarm must be broken. It COULDN'T be morning already. But it was. Reality, aided by stiff pokes in both of their ribs, soon broke through the fuzzy twilight and they fell out of bed to fight over the bathroom.

Showered, coffeed and feeling almost human again, Richie and Freemo set out for the train station in the cab the girls had thoughtfully remembered to order for them.

It was a cold, grey morning as their train arrived in Middlesbrough. Stuart was already there, well wrapped up against the northern chill. "Fucking buffet's not open yet" he observed. "And I've done a recce. The pubs round here don't open for nearly an hour either". He looked glum. Bollocks! How could they do to kill an hour? Middlesbrough was quite often a rough place to go and there was a big chance that they would be picked off before the main Tottenham support arrived.

Sure enough, as they exited the concourse, a suspicious looking guy in a Celtic shirt was positioned on the opposite side of the road. As they emerged, he casually produced his mobile and began making a few calls. Now it MAY have been that the calls were entirely innocent, but the three lads weren't taking any chances, diving through crowded shops and doubling back on their tracks; eventually shaking off what became apparent was an attempted tail by the Celt.

They found themselves outside an open fish and chip shop at about ten thirty (my God the chippies open early up North!). With nothing better to do, they decided on a chip breakfast. Might soak up some of the beer they hoped they would soon be drinking. The owner of the chippie was probably Italian. He MAY have been a local, but anyhow the lads found it fucking difficult to understand more than the odd word of his conversation.

Aware of the potential for trouble, the lads asked him if he could direct them to a pub which met their four essential criteria:- Not too near to (or too far from) the Ayresome Park ground. About a mile might do. Not a Middlesbrough fans drinker. A decent / smart pub – not too rough. From his response, the lads distilled that they should head for a nice pub called the Empire. Did food end everything. Not FAR from the ground, but more of a gastro pub really. Never known any trouble there, he hadn't.

And so, having polished off the last of their greasy breakfasts, the lads hailed a stray black cab and asked for the Empire. No sign of the Celt and his mates.

The cab dropped the friends off outside the pub and they were pleasantly surprised as they pushed through the double doors into the only just opened boozer. In fact the word boozer did it an injustice – it was quite posh really. Red velour seats with no discernable rips. Brass handrails. A decent food menu. No graffiti to speak of in the bogs. The Empire was a large pub but the friends were the only three in it for quite a while.

On the third round, Stuey spotted the quiz machine and suggested they pass some time playing it. Being nice and cosy inside, the lads piled their coats on the floor by the machine and began feeding it.

166

Three quid at a time. They changed button man at frequent intervals as in turn they failed the 'don't fucking press it unless you're absolutely sure' test.

At first they won a little – all three were intelligent lads and each seemed to know bits that the others didn't. And the prizes were in cash. But gradually the lagers kicked in and somehow the wrong buttons were pressed much more often.

Engrossed in the questions the lads got double rounds in – six pints at a time. Without them noticing, the pub had begun to fill up, but there seemed no threat in such a middle class, steak-night-out-with-the-missus type pub.

Until that is, the tap on Freemo's shoulder. He looked round – and down – at the little guy who was smiling innocently enough. "Excuse me boys" he began politely, "would you be from London?". The accent was unmistakeably north-eastern. The lads exchanged glances. He didn't wait for an answer before he carried on "Because I've been working on the bricks down in Wood Green. Do you know Wood Green?".

Freemo was first to gather his wits. "No mate" he replied using the Worcester accent he had long ago lost. "We're actually from the Midlands. Just here to see relatives". Well, it was mostly true – he and Richie WERE born in the Midlands. And Richie and Stuart WERE seeing relatives..

"Nay worry lads!" he smiled. "I won't tell them you're Cockneys". As he spoke, he nodded backwards over his shoulder. The lads followed his nod and – to their horror – now noticed that the pub had filled up whilst they had been playing the quiz. With skinheaded, booted, tattooed Boro fans. Some of whom were fucking huge. All of whom were staring directly at them.

"No mate, we're not" Freemo insisted, his Midland accent becoming stronger still. "We're from Worcester actually".

"Don't worry mate, I won't tell them anyhow" smirked the brickie as he began sauntering back to the assembled mob of at least two hundred scowling Boro lads.

Urgent, whispered discussions broke out. The lads decided to brass it out and continued to play the machine. But every time they casually looked round, old Wood Green was laughing and pointing them out to his mates.

Fuck it – we're about to get out heads kicked in here!" Freemo hissed. Stuart agreed. Even Richie appeared to. "What we do is wait until something interesting comes on the tele, grab our coats and run like fuck!" Freemo said. The others nodded in agreement. It seemed the only way out.

Deciding that they couldn't hear the TV properly anyhow, they made their move. Stuart and Freemo snatched their coats off the floor and thrust Richie's at him. They moved fast towards the double doors. Richie got one arm into his jacket until his military training came to the fore and he changed his mind. "Fuck 'em!" he roared. "Let's have a go!". Stuart and Freemo dragged him, punching and kicking, through the swing doors as the Boro lads attacked.

No one knew how or why, but as the three spilled out onto the street, Old Bill was outside with a large German Shepherd police dog. In fact a fucking huge one. As the doors swung to and fro, the Boro mob stopped dead in their tracks when confronted by the snarling canine.

This bought the lads just enough time. They sprinted to the end of the road and pile into a passing cab, panting. By now the Boro boys had braved up again and had swarmed past the overwhelmed Policeman in pursuit.

"Where to lads?" asked the smiling cabbie.

"Anywhere but fucking here! Quick!" came the three simultaneous replies.

The cabbie suddenly noticed the fast approaching mob, now only yards away, and burst into action. Have you ever seen wheel spin in a black cab? Away they shot, in the nick of time. The cabbie did three

168

laps round the block and – ten minutes later – dropped the shaken three off in exactly the same place as he had picked them up! Thankfully, the Police had restored order – there were four dogs and a horse outside the pub. Otherwise the street was empty. Thank fuck.

The lads warily made their way, via a side street – to the football ground. Once safely inside the away fans section, relief began to surface. Except for Richie. "Nah – we should've given them a better go" he insisted.

Yes mate. Just shut the fuck up.

FOOTNOTE: A colleague of Freemo's happened to be at the game with his son. He was a Wolves fan and just wanted to watch a game whilst he was in the area. His tickets were in the Boro end. He was threatened for being a suspected Cockney. By a guy in a Celtic shirt. After the game, Richie and Freemo went back to Newcastle, pissed. They went out for a meal with the girls and Suzanne's Mum. Then on to a city centre club, where a large fight broke out. Nothing to do with them. Sadly, both Suzanne's Mum and Gran died suddenly in the following closed season. Brain tumours, Freemo was told.

Result : Middlesbrough. 2 – 2 Tottenham Hotspur (Stewart (2))

Attendance ; 23,692

169

Oh and by the way...

~

Hollins had moved to America to follow his girlfriend, Kim. Kim was a nurse. She was fed up with Pete and left him behind. Pete followed on. He found it difficult to get jobs…. first he was a cactus cutter; next he was a janitor in a block of 'condos'.

Things didn't work out with Kim. And then U.S. immigration caught up with him an put him in a camp ready for expulsion. His girlfriend Jennie visited him there and – a few days before he had to leave – proposed to him.

As they were married, Hollins could stay indefinitely. Bit by bit he got a foothold on the job ladder and, by the time he decided to come home, he had made it to Food and Beverage Director at the Sheraton in El Paso. Freemo reckoned the stocks would be well down when they checked!

Sadly, things didn't work out for Pete with Jennie either. By then his drinking was out of control and he had an eating disorder too. Jennie started seeing another bloke and left. And that fucked Pete up completely. R.I.P. mate.

~

CHAPTER THIRTEEN

CRYSTAL PALACE AWAY
A BIT OF A RUMBLE
(18/11/1989)

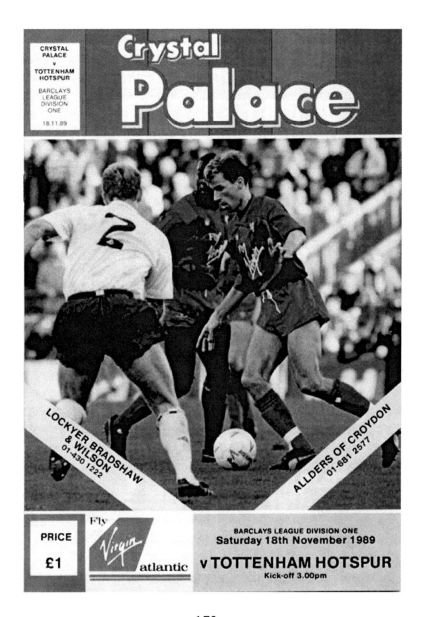

Palace away was always one to look forward to. Yes, transport was crap but there were a few good pubs near to the ground and Tottenham always took thousands of fans to support the team.

Freemo made his way down from Amersham, via Baker Street, Victoria and Selhurst. Only stopping for a quick beer whilst waiting for the stopping train out of Victoria. The bar there was already packed with Spurs fans and Ian – one of his regular drinking buddies from the British Queen and the Railway Tavern and widely known as Hustle – tapped him on the shoulder as he pushed through the crowd to get a beer. Theresa and Doyley were in there too. 'Tree' a pretty blonde girl from Southend, had been going since she was a teenager and knew Freemo from the British Queen days. He bought a round and told them the time of the next train to Selhurst. They had twelve minutes and so quickly swigged away their beers to catch it.

Nearly missed it too. Had to run for it. But soon they settled into ripped seats for the twenty five minute journey through the graffiti covered jungles of South East London. Those from North London look down their noses at South London, particularly SE. Shit-hole. Those from there look on North Londoners with similar disdain. Ponces.

Soon enough the train pulled into Selhurst station. They could have used Thornton Heath, but this one suited better for the pubs they were meeting friends in. The friends walked quickly through the rows of terraced houses, past the ground with the weird semi circular roof and on to the Ship pub. About a ten to fifteen minute walk was all but Ian huffed and puffed and moaned at the walk. He had had an accident when he was younger which left him with a slight limp. No one but the Old Bill actually noticed it, but that was unfortunate. On two occasions he had been nicked as he walked unsteadily up to away grounds. Charged with trying to gain entrance to a football ground whilst pissed he was. And found guilty, but that's another story.

Freemo and Theresa pushed on into the pub as Doyley got the door for Hustle. The Ship was a long, thin pub and despite it still being before midday, the bar was already crowded with away fans.

The group of Londoners that Freemo had arranged to meet had chosen the pub. Well Orpington Dave had actually, largely because they sold Pukka pies…. and he loved them. You wouldn't believe this guy had run the London Marathon – and finished in a respectable enough time.

Anyhow, there was Dave, perched on a stool next to the pie warming display. And Sledge, Shaun, Ian and the others. They all knew Hustle, Tree and Doyley and the group slipped quickly into round buying. Sledge had arranged to meet Steve Sedgley (not the real one, but a builder who looked exactly like him and drank in the Corner Pin in Tottenham) at a pub round the corner and so – because drinks were taking an age to be served and the pies had run out – a large group of friends walked round the corner to the Portmanor. Via the Bounty for a quick one. Well, it seemed rude to pass a pub, didn't it.

The Portmanor was largish pub, back under the railway bridge. It was now after one o'clock and, whilst a lot of white shirts made the pub busy, it wasn't as crowded as the Ship, which was mobbed by the time they had left it. There were a few Palace lads in there too, but they were certainly nothing to worry about. Palace were regarded as a bit of a joke club by the North Londoners. Sure, they had a bit of a firm, but nothing much.

Gary the postman and his wife Alison came over and joined the round, which by now was up to around a dozen drinkers. It seemed sensible to split into two groups and so that's what happened. Gary didn't have a match ticket. The friends asked around for him, but there wasn't much about…. and those tickets that WERE on offer were going for too much money.

Sedge arrived with a big bag of tools – he'd been laying bricks in the area that morning and had had to come straight from work. He asked the barman if the bag could be left at the pub whilst the game was on and permission was granted. Result! They'd have to come back after to collect them! Good excuse for a few post match beers then.

The singing began as the beers took effect. Nothing specific to Crystal Palace…. but lots slagging the Goons, West Ham and Chelsea. Most singing Tottenham's praises.

Dave disappeared to the chip shop for another pie to keep his blood sugar levels up, but otherwise the friends all stayed together until around half two when they began to drift away to the match. By this time the Portmanor had filled to bursting with Spurs fans. Gary still hadn't managed to get a reasonably priced ticket and had resigned himself to staying in the pub drinking. At least there was a tele which would have score flashes. And the lads would be back in two hours to continue the party. Nah, it wasn't so bad. Tree and Doyley regularly went to away games and did the same thing. Just being part of the crowd was sometimes enough.

Freemo, Hustle, Tree and Doyley were last to leave and had to hurry towards the ground. Ian was well pissed by this time and the limp accentuated the effect. Freemo and Doyley spotted the Old Bill eyeing him up as they approached the turnstiles.

Tree acted quickly and linked arms with him, steadying him and making it seem he was part of a couple. Much less likely to cause trouble if the missus was with you. And so the Police parted and let all of them in with no more than a cursory frisking.

The Arthur Waite stand was full from front to back with Tottenham fans – a great turn out as always. The teams were already on the pitch and one by one acknowledged the fans as their names were chanted in turn. The singing echoed loudly from the roof of the old grandstand as the game kicked off.

The Spurs fans had high hopes of an easy win. Gary Lineker was the league's top scorer and was bang in form. Hopefully he could knock in a couple. Moreover, Palace hadn't beaten Spurs in a competitive game throughout the 1980s. And they had only been promoted back to the top flight that season. No, it should have been an easy victory.

But things didn't exactly go to plan. Palace put up a good fight and the game to'd and fro'd. Tottenham did manage to run out winners by the odd goal in five, but it was disappointingly close.

The lads weren't kept in after the game by the Police, who were working on the assumption that there were far too many of them for Palace fans to attack. There had even been Spurs fans in all areas of the ground as well as the officially allocated away section. So they reckoned that if it was going to kick off, it would have done so long ago. So the friends walked back to the Portmanor, bought Gary a drink, gave him a match programme and proceeded to moan about the game. You'd have though Spurs had lost!

The pub again filled with Spurs fans – maybe a couple of hundred of them. Not all were in the same grumpy mood and so the friends soon joined in the singing as they ordered and swigged away at more beers. There were Palace fans in there too, but they sat quietly in a little group at the bar. The drinking went on and the crowd began to thin out. Tree and Doyley had initially had to sit on the stairs and it seemed they were comfortable there. Gary and Alison left. Orpington Dave disappeared in search of a pie.

All pissed by now, the lads hadn't noticed just how empty the pub had become. It was just their group of about eight…. and the twenty or so Palace boys who had, by now, begun to find their voices. Well if you can call hissing a voice. Things were quickly getting nasty – the hissing was meant to be the sound of gas chambers; a not-too-subtle reference to Tottenham's Jewish links.

For one reason or another, the Palace firm had taken a dislike to Freemo. Maybe because he was the biggest. Maybe because he was singing loudly earlier. He didn't know. But the 'leader' of the Palace was offering him out by gesticulating across the room. The odds were not in their favour – more than two to one against. Freemo declined. Sedge is a six footer too, but not of a particularly big build. He approached Freemo, though, and suggested the two of them took on the twenty Palace. "Nah" said Freemo simply, and walked straight past the Palace group into the Gents. He ignored them. They sneered at him.

As he made space for a few more beers, he half expected the door to burst open and the Palace fans to pile into him. But, as it turned out, they had their hands full out in the pub.

When he re-emerged into the bar area, he found everyone standing up. And lots of shouting going on. His eyes quickly scanned round the pub. And that's when he saw Sedge, his head tucked firmly under the arm of the Palace 'leader'. Apparently they had hissed again, he had seen red and stormed the fucking lot of them. On his own.

Seeing his predicament, Freemo felt obliged to help and so he bounced over and smacked they guy who had hold of Sedge firmly in the head. In one way it had the desired effect. The guy staggered backwards and let go of Sedge. On the other hand the other Palace fans were now looking distinctly fucking annoyed with the two of them! Time to go. Freemo and Sedge turned their backs, went back to their group and suggested it was time to leave. Quickly. Tree finished her pint. Freemo got a clump in the back of the head, but the expected riot didn't break out.

The friends spilled out onto the footpath, turning to face any aggressors. But Sedge had realised he'd forgotten his builders tools and had gone back inside through another door. Doyley, who hadn't really got involved was still inside trying to calm things down. He and Sedge suddenly burst back out onto the street again - Sedge was still fucking annoyed.

The group of friends outside had dwindled. Sledge had begun to make his way back to the station, as had a couple of others. His foreign office job was at stake. Sedge began handing out large and sharp building tools to Freemo and Doyley. "Fuck 'em" he raged. "If they come outside let's have 'em!".

Freemo clutched the six foot spirit level. Doyley looked quizzically at the large trowel in his hand. The three stood shoulder to shoulder in the middle of the road, waiting for the row. And, for some inexplicable reason, it never came!

Whether the landlord stopped them coming out; whether they were a little bit worried by the mad blokes in the middle of the road waving brickies implements; whether they just couldn't be bothered.... No-one had a scooby. But it was probably just as well in the circumstances.

Result: Crystal Palace 2 – 3 Tottenham (Howells, Samways, Lineker (pen))

Attendance: 25,366

Oh and by the way...

~

After a two week camping holiday in France, Freemo, his brother Nigel (Freemo junior) and their partners were reading the English papers on the early morning ferry home. They noticed that Tottenham's first team was due to play a cricket match in Cheshunt the following day, versus the Hoddesdon and District chamber of commerce. As it was Saturday, they decided it would be a good idea to go to the game and travel back to Worcester afterwards.

And so it was that the four pulled into the Spurs training ground and set up camping tables and chairs on the boundary.

Turned out to be a great day. Al Sutt – a good mate from London had also turned out and was amazed to see the Midlanders cooking bacon sarnies on the boundary.

No-one can remember much about the actual game, except Mark Falco opened the batting and scored a half century.

Freemo still treasures the programme as perhaps the most unusual one he ever owned (see over).

~

CHARITY CRICKET MATCH

HODDESDON
& DISTRICT
CHAMBER OF
COMMERCE

v

SPURS
FIRST TEAM

PRICE 20p

CHAPTER FOURTEEN

Q.P.R. AWAY
KIDNAPPING THE POLE
(17/3/1990)

Freemo and his new wife Julie made their way from Amersham by tube for this one. Met. line to Baker Street then change for Shepherds Bush. He didn't bother with cans for the journey, as it was still early and he was expecting a big day on the drink with the mates he was meeting.

The ancient tube train rattled and creaked through North West London and the pair read the tabloids as they passed Wembley's twin towers without as much as a sideways glance.

Baker Street can be confusing to people who don't use it much, because of an over complex system of stairs, bridges and tunnels. But Freemo and Julie negotiated the change without thinking. And soon they were walking down the steps of Shepherd's Bush tube station. Early.

Today they were meeting three sets of friends – firstly Richie Rich, Phil, Stuart and a few others from West Drayton and also some of the Worcester lads. Later they were meeting Sledge, Shaun, Orpington Dave and the boys with whom the after match drinking would probably drag on into the evening.

But it was still too early and, with an hour to kill, the two turned into Shepherd's Bush market for a poke around. Two rows of stalls lining the wide gap between shops on either side. Good for everything from a snack through to expensive colour graduated jumpers with aeroplanes on. Some of it knocked off, some of it useless tat, but interesting sights and smells all the same. There were worse ways to pass the time.

Glancing at his watch, Freemo realised it was not far off opening time and that they were still about ten minutes walk away from the Springbok pub where he had arranged to meet the West London Spurs lads. They crossed the Uxbridge Road and set off at a brisk pace in the direction of the ground. Before reaching it, they veered right and through blocks of run down council flats, emerging at the back into one of those concrete squares surrounded by the usual council estate shops – a chippy, a bookie, a seven-eleven convenience store, an offie and a newsagent. But there was also the Springbok pub – a run down,

186

shitty sort of place but they always got served there and it always seemed to be full of Tottenham fans on match days. Not that there was any worry about Q.P.R. They didn't really have a firm to talk about. Their 'end' was the Loft and most away fans took it at will. No, there was never any trouble at Rangers – it was always a bloody good day out.

As they approached, the small waiting crowd disappeared into the pub as it opened its doors so they joined on to the end and waited in line for their drinks.

Before they had been served, Phil and Richie came in, tapped Freemo on the shoulder and ordered a couple of pints. And before they had been handed them, in walked Stevesham, Sensible Keith, Cowboy and a few more from Worcester. It was turning into an expensive round! Eventually Freemo managed to get all the beers ordered and paid for and the group made their way back outside onto the concreted area. It was a lovely day in early spring and it seemed much nicer to be outside than inside the grimy, smokey bar.

Dennis the Hat (one of the Uxbridge lads) had a tip for a horse. He knew the owner and he was having a big punt on it himself. Good enough for Freemo, who went straight into the bookies and put twenty quid on it. Some of the other lads had a dabble too – Dennis usually knew what he was talking about when it came to the horses.

As usual, the discussions revolved around the team, the tactics and general opinions on who had been crap and who had in recent weeks. Spurs had won three-nil at Charlton the week before but the previous three games had all been lost to smaller teams (Aston Villa, Derby County and Crystal Palace). Worse still, Tottenham had only managed one goal (from a midfielder) in those three matches. Which Tottenham would turn up today, they wondered?

The rounds of beers flowed. More and more Spurs fans turned up and swelled the crowd in the square... and the queue at the bar. Some lads grabbed a fish and chip lunch, others a burger from the handily parked van. But eating and betting didn't interrupt the constant stream of beers they enjoyed in the sunshine.

A few home fans had showed up in ones and twos, but there was no trouble. They just stood and drank with the Spurs lads.

The lads went into the bookies to watch Dennis's horse run, and sure enough it won, easily and at good odds of 8/1. Freemo was over a hundred and fifty quid better off. That was the last beer Dennis was going to have to buy that day!

Fuelled up and happy, the friends made the short walk to the ground at quarter to three. Freemo and Julie's tickets were in with the visiting fans, some of the others had tickets in the main stand and one or two were going in 'the Loft' for a row. Which didn't materialise as there were very few Q.P.R. fans there for them to fight with.

The game itself was another let down. Spurs played poorly and, apart from a goal from Paul Walsh, hardly had a shot on target in yet another defeat to a small club. Tottenham lost 1-3 and Freemo left before the final whistle, disgusted.

He and Julie made their way back to the White Lion pub on the other side of the Uxbridge Road. There were bouncers on the door now, but Julie's presence put them at ease and they let the pair in with no problems. They took a seat near the window so they could spot their friends as they arrived.

As it often does on nice Spring days, it had become very cold outside by now. The warmth of the pub caused condensation on the inside of the windows.

Soon afterwards Orpington Dave, Sledge and his cousin Shaun arrived with three or four others. Despite the bad result, the new arrivals were in high spirits and ready for a party. Freemo was still sulking, but they soon snapped him out of it. The drinking quickly gathered pace and the area near the window was soon filled with laughter.

Dave happened to notice a strange looking older bloke outside. Stranger still, he appeared to be trying to wipe the condensation off the window... from outside!!!! The doormen were eyeing him warily and it looked like he wasn't going to get in. Freemo spotted the Spurs badge on his lapel and sprung into action. He went outside, smiling at the bouncers as he went and grabbed the startled bloke by the arm. "Ah THERE you are, Dad!" he said loudly. "Come on – we've got you a pint in. Where HAVE you been?".

The bouncers moved aside and let the pair through, even with the older guy looking distinctly bewildered.

So they didn't all get thrown out, someone bought the guy a pint and insisted he sat with them for at least a few minutes. Turned out he was a Polish bloke called Paul Heller. He'd had a row with his wife so he'd gone to the game and got pretty pissed. He didn't seem keen to go home and conversed with the friends in broken English, quickly warming to them. Trying to join in on the quick banter. Failing.

But he stayed, was bought a few free beers and listened to the advice from the lads.

"Fuck her off mate – she shouldn't be able to make you feel like this" said Shaun.

"Stay out for a day or two – she'll soon appreciate you!" offered Freemo. Julie glared hard at him.

Paul Heller, it seemed, had already made up his mind to go home and apologise, although he wasn't sure what for. Meanwhile, the lads were becoming bored and had decided to move on to the West End for cocktails. As there were now eleven of them, three black cabs were ordered. The Polish guy declined the invitation to join them, despite severe pressure. An idea began to hatch amongst the friends.

The first taxi arrived and the first group of four went outside.

"Aren't you going to say goodbye to them, Paul?" asked Dave, apparently innocently.

Mr Heller went outside to shake hands with the generous lads.... and found himself bundled into the cab. He struggled but it was no good. The driver showed a little surprise, but pulled out into the traffic and headed for the Long Island cocktail bar in Lower St. Martins Lane. Paul

Heller, it seemed, was a bit pissed by now and just sat there looking bewildered.

The other two cabs quickly followed the first and soon the ten mates, a tutting Julie and a confused Pole were installed at a table at the back of the room in the already busy cocktail bar.

Sledge organised a twenty-quid-a-man whip round. The lads agreed to exempt Mr Heller. And soon the first round of 'Attitude Adjusters' appeared on their table. For anyone who likes cocktails, they're Long Island Iced Teas with an extra white spirit added. They still tasted like cola but were fucking lethal! Heller sipped his with a worried, distasteful look on his face.

"You enjoy yourself mate. That'll fucking show her!" remarked Shaun.

"But I have get home now", replied the Pole. "She worry and I no want that. Really I love. I very pissed now".

The lads bought him another cocktail, but he just ignored it. He was getting boring now.

"You'd better fuck off home then" said someone disinterestedly. "Where is it you live Paul?".

"Above White Horse pub" he slurred back.

Not only had the lads dragged him into his own home, they had then kidnapped him from it!

The friends took money from the kitty and poured the Pole into a cab home to Shepherds Bush. The divorce probably went through soon after.

Result : Q.P.R. 3 – 1 Tottenham Hotspur (Walsh)

Attendance : 16,691

THE LADS NOWADAYS (2009)

Freemo is now 54. He split up with Julie and later had another failed marriage (another Julie). He was successful at work and ended up as Managing Director of a London marketing company. He now lives happily in Devon doing a bit of this and that with his third wife Sarah. He has held a season ticket for the past 21 years and has maintained regular support of his beloved Spurs.

His brother Nigel (Freemo jnr.) died on April 11th 2002 aged 40, having had problems with drugs and drink. He left two children – Em and Jack - behind. They both follow Spurs.

Hollins died in January 2008, aged 52, after a long fight against alcoholic illness. In the 1980s he went to the United States – El Paso - to follow his girlfriend Kim and stayed there 8 years but it didn't work out and he later married an American, Jen. That didn't work either. He returned to Worcester, where for some time he ran pubs with his partner Bid. His Mum, Ivy, died a few years ago.

Smiffy is 54, married and is living in Upton, Worcestershire. He still works in the printing industry and is married to Gail, after a couple of failed attempts. Nowadays he goes two or three games each season. He's still driving too – never been banned and goes a bit slower nowadays. Smiffy stayed close mates with Freemo and Hollins.

Spence has also turned 50 and is still happily married to Pauline and still lives in Worcester. They have four children. He doesn't go to games any more, but has the occasional drink with the lads. Spence is a golfer nowadays.

Glenn Moore is 54 and last time anyone heard from him he was a successful barrister in London, working with commercial and shipping law. The mooring of ships maybe? They haven't seen him at the football for years, or back in Worcester. He's moving in higher circles now. Good luck to him.

AND THEIR MATES

Pricey now lives back in Worcester with his wife and family, after moving to Cyprus for two years in 2004. The Cowboy lives and works in Worcester and still travels regularly to games as a season ticket holder. He appeared in a TV ad once, showing off the Spurs tattoo on his stomach. The football looks more like a rugby ball nowadays.

PG lives in Birmingham, but finds it difficult to go to games after redundancy from his job with Rover. Goof has had his teeth fixed, the sack from his job and he hasn't been to a game for over twenty years. Duncan Mac now lives in Australia. His marriage broke up soon after he emigrated.

The Buzzes have ditched their bobble hats, still live in Worcester and rarely go anymore. Nor Crowbar. Nor Stick.

Paul Hollins moved to New Zealand, but it didn't work out. He's back in Worcester now and he still goes to quite a few games as does his brother Phil.

Shaun is married and has a Tottenham supporting son called Chris. He owns a chain of shops in Majorca, from where he still manages to attend a few games each year. Brendan's whereabouts are unknown.

Paddington Billy spent a few years in prison for an assault with a pickaxe handle, came out and fell off a roof. He walks with a stick now.

Of the three Micks from Warrington, Micky D. has moved to Majorca — and back. He still goes to games. Mick Mac died in 2003 after a short illness. Micky W. recovered from throat cancer and is now a University lecturer, living in Coventry. He still goes to the occasional home game and on European trips.

Freemo still remains firm friends with the Jersey couple he met at his wedding in 1989, Mick and Majella.

Al Sutt is now a postman in Liverpool.

Aidy from Coventry died some time ago.

Sget, the Lincoln goalie, was killed in a minibus crash.

The lads lost touch with Tommy Hall and heard two stories about his whereabouts nowadays. The first account, sadly, is that Tommy became alcoholic and died. The second is that, whilst he is alcoholic, he is working as a baker. Let's hope you're baking bread Tommy mate.

A COMPLETE RECORD OF TOTTENHAM HOTSPUR FIXTURES
THROUGHOUT THE 1980s

(produced by kind permission of Jim Duggan – www.topspurs.com)

1980 - 1981 – Manager Keith Burkinshaw

Season 1980-1981	Played	Won	Drew	Lost	For	Agst.	Points
Division 1 - 10th	42	14	15	13	70	68	57
F.A. Cup -Winners	9	6	3	0	19	7	Winners
League Cup	6	4	1	1	8	3	5th Rnd
Total - Season 1980-1981	57	24	19	14	97	78	10th

Tottenham Hotspur in the League - Season 1980-1981

16-Aug-80 Division 1	43,398 H Nottingham Forest	W	2	-	0	Hoddle(pen), Crooks
19-Aug-80 Division 1	27,841 A Crystal Palace	W	4	-	3	Archibald, Hoddle, Crooks (2)
23-Aug-80 Division 1	39,763 H Brighton & HA	D	2	-	2	Hoddle, Crooks
30-Aug-80 Division 1	54,054 A Arsenal	L	0	-	2	
06-Sep-80 Division 1	40,995 H Manchester United	D	0	-	0	
13-Sep-80 Division 1	21,947 A Leeds United	D	0	-	0	
20-Sep-80 Division 1	32,030 H Sunderland	D	0	-	0	
27-Sep-80 Division 1	22,616 A Leicester City	L	1	-	2	Villa
04-Oct-80 Division 1	18,614 A Stoke City	W	3	-	2	Hughton, Archibald, Taylor (pen)
11-Oct-80 Division 1	27,380 H Middlesbrough	W	3	-	2	Archibald, Villa, Crooks
18-Oct-80 Division 1	30,940 A Aston Villa	L	0	-	3	
22-Oct-80 Division 1	28,788 A Manchester City	L	1	-	3	Hoddle

199

Date	Division	Venue/Opponent	Res	Score	Scorers
25-Oct-80	Division 1	25,484 H Coventry City	W	4 - 1	Archibald (2), Hoddle (2)
01-Nov-80	Division 1	26,223 A Everton	D	2 - 2	Archibald (2)
08-Nov-80	Division 1	29,244 H Wolves	D	2 - 2	Hoddle(pen), Crooks
12-Nov-80	Division 1	25,777 H Crystal Palace	W	4 - 2	Archibald, Crooks (3)
15-Nov-80	Division 1	25,400 A Nottingham Forest	W	3 - 0	Ardiles, Archibald (2)
22-Nov-80	Division 1	24,817 A Birmingham City	L	1 - 2	Ardiles
29-Nov-80	Division 1	27,372 H West Bromwich Albion	L	2 - 3	Lacy, Perryman
06-Dec-80	Division 1	39,545 A Liverpool	L	1 - 2	Archibald
13-Dec-80	Division 1	23,883 H Manchester City	W	2 - 1	Archibald, Hoddle
17-Dec-80	Division 1	22,741 H Ipswich Town	W	5 - 3	Perryman, Ardiles, Archibald, Hoddle, Crooks
20-Dec-80	Division 1	15,990 A Middlesbrough	L	1 - 4	Lacy
26-Dec-80	Division 1	28,792 H Southampton	D	4 - 4	Brooke (2), Archibald, Crooks
27-Dec-80	Division 1	23,145 A Norwich City	D	2 - 2	Archibald, Hoddle
10-Jan-81	Division 1	24,909 H Birmingham City	W	1 - 0	Crooks
17-Jan-81	Division 1	32,944 H Arsenal	W	2 - 0	Archibald (2)
31-Jan-81	Division 1	23,610 A Brighton & HA	W	2 - 0	Ardiles, Crooks
07-Feb-81	Division 1	32,372 H Leeds United	D	1 - 1	Archibald
17-Feb-81	Division 1	40,642 A Manchester United	D	0 - 0	
21-Feb-81	Division 1	27,326 H Leicester City	L	1 - 2	Archibald
28-Feb-81	Division 1	22,382 A Sunderland	D	1 - 1	Crooks
11-Mar-81	Division 1	28,742 H Stoke City	D	2 - 2	Ardiles, Brooke

14-Mar-81	Division 1	32,044	A	Ipswich Town	L	0 - 3	
21-Mar-81	Division 1	35,091	H	Aston Villa	W	2 - 0	Archibald, Crooks
28-Mar-81	Division 1	18,654	A	Coventry City	W	1 - 0	Roberts og
04-Apr-81	Division 1	27,208	H	Everton	D	2 - 2	Galvin, Crooks
18-Apr-81	Division 1	34,413	H	Norwich City	L	2 - 3	Miller, Hoddle (pen)
20-Apr-81	Division 1	23,735	A	Southampton	D	1 - 1	Miller
25-Apr-81	Division 1	35,334	H	Liverpool	D	1 - 1	Hoddle
30-Apr-81	Division 1	18,350	A	Wolves	L	0 - 1	
02-May-81	Division 1	20,549	A	West Bromwich Albion	L	2 - 4	Smith, Falco

Tottenham Hotspur in the FA Cup - Season 1980-1981   WINNERS

03-Jan-81	F.A. Cup 3	28,829	A	Queens Park Rangers	D	0 - 0	
07-Jan-81	F.A. Cup 3	36,294	H	Queens Park Rangers	W	3 - 1	Galvin, Hoddle, Crooks
24-Jan-81	F.A. Cup 4	37,532	H	Hull City	W	2 - 0	Archibald, Brooke
14-Feb-81	F.A. Cup 5	36,688	H	Coventry City	W	3 - 1	Hughton, Ardiles, Archibald
07-Mar-81	F.A. Cup 6	40,629	H	Exeter City	W	2 - 0	Miller, Roberts
11-Apr-81	F.A. Cup SF	40,174	HI	Wolves	D	2 - 2	Archibald, Hoddle
15-Apr-81	F.A. Cup SF	52,539	Hi	Wolves	W	3 - 0	Crooks (2), Villa
09-May-81	F.A. Cup Final	100,000	W	Manchester City	D	1 - 1	Hutchinson og
14-May-81	F.A. Cup Final	96,000	W	Manchester City	W	3 - 2	Villa(2), Crooks

201

Tottenham Hotspur in the League Cup - Season 1980-1981

27-Aug-80 L.C. Cup 2 (1L)	20,087	A	Orient	W	1 - 0	Lacy
03-Sep-80 L.C. Cup 2 (2L)	25,806	H	Orient	W	3 - 1	Archibald (2), Crooks
24-Sep-80 L.C. Cup 3	29,654	H	Crystal Palace	D	0 - 0	
30-Sep-80 L.C. Cup 3	26,885	A	Crystal Palace	W	3 - 1	Villa, Hoddle, Crooks
04-Nov-80 L.C. Cup 4	42,511	H	Arsenal	W	1 - 0	Ardiles
02-Dec-80 L.C. Cup 5	36,003	A	West Ham United	L	0 - 1	

Tottenham Hotspur - Friendly Matches - Season 1980-1981

28-Jul-80 Friendly	-	A	Southend United	D 1 - 1	Archibald
30-Jul-80 Friendly	-	A	Portsmouth	W 2 - 1	Hughton, Falco
02-Aug-80 Friendly	-	A	PSV Eindhoven	L 2 - 4	Ardiles, Taylor
04-Aug-80 Friendly	-	A	Glasgow Rangers	L 1 - 2	Lacy
05-Aug-80 Friendly	-	A	Dundee United	L 1 - 4	Crooks
08-Aug-80 Friendly	-	A	Swansea City	L 0 - 1	
17-Nov-80 Friendly	-	A	Weymouth	W 6 - 1	Ardiles (2), Villa(2), Gibson, Dyer og
02-Feb-81 Friendly	-	A	Jersey Select XI	W 5 - 0	Ardiles, Archibald (3), Brooke
11-May-81 Friendly/Test		H	West Ham United	L 2 - 3	Hazard, Gibson
Barry Daines Testimonial					

Tottenham Hotspur Tour - Bahrain, Kuwait & Turkey - Summer 1981

Date		Opponent	Result	Scorers
20-May-81 Tour	- A	Syrian Police	W 4 - 0	Holmes, Falco, Taylor (2)
24-May-81 Tour	- A	Bahrain Select XI	W 3 - 0	Miller, Galvin, Brooke
26-May-81 Tour	- A	Kuwait Army XI	W 2 - 1	Brooke, Crooks
28-May-81 Tour	- A	Bahrain Select XI	W 5 - 3	Miller, Galvin, Falco (2), Crooks
19-Jun-81 Tour	- A	Trabzonspor	W 4 - 0	Villa, Ardiles, Falco, Crooks
23-Jun-81 Tour	- A	Fenerbahche	W 5 - 1	Villa, Falco, Galvin, Hoddle, Crooks

1981 - 1982 – Manager Keith Burkinshaw

Season 1981-1982	Played	Won	Drew	Lost	For	Agst.	Points
Division 1 - 4th	42	20	11	11	67	48	71
F.A. Cup – Winners	7	6	1	0	10	3	Winners
League Cup - Runners Up	8	6	1	1	8	3	RunnersUp
European Cup Winners Cup	8	4	2	2	12	6	SemiFinal
Charity Shield (Aston Villa)	1	0	1	0	2	2	Shared
Total - Season 1981-1982	66	36	16	14	99	62	4th

Tottenham Hotspur in the League - Season 1981-1982

29-Aug-81	Division 1	20,490	A	Middlesbrough	W 3 - 1 Villa, Hoddle, Falco
02-Sep-81	Division 1	41,200	H	West Ham United	L 0 - 4
05-Sep-81	Division 1	31,265	H	Aston Villa	L 1 - 3 Villa
12-Sep-81	Division 1	18,675	A	Wolves	W 1 - 0 Galvin
19-Sep-81	Division 1	31,219	H	Everton	W 3 - 0 Hughton, Roberts, Hoddle (pen)
22-Sep-81	Division 1	22,352	A	Swansea City	L 1 - 2 Hoddle (pen)
26-Sep-81	Division 1	39,085	A	Manchester City	W 1 - 0 Falco
03-Oct-81	Division 1	34,870	H	Nottingham Forest	W 3 - 0 Hazard, Falco (2)
10-Oct-81	Division 1	30,520	H	Stoke City	W 2 - 0 Ardiles, Crooks
17-Oct-81	Division 1	25,317	A	Sunderland	W 2 - 0 Hazard, Archibald

Date	Competition	Attendance	H/A	Opponent	Result	Scorers
24-Oct-81	Division 1	37,294	H	Brighton & HA	L 0 - 1	
31-Oct-81	Division 1	24,131	A	Southampton	W 2 - 1	Roberts, Corbett
07-Nov-81	Division 1	32,436	H	West Bromwich Albion	L 1 - 2	Crooks
21-Nov-81	Division 1	35,534	H	Manchester United	W 3 - 1	Roberts, Hazard, Archibald
28-Nov-81	Division 1	15,550	A	Notts County	D 2 - 2	Crooks (2)
05-Dec-81	Division 1	27,972	H	Coventry City	L 1 - 2	Hazard
12-Dec-81	Division 1	28,780	A	Leeds United	D 0 - 0	
27-Jan-82	Division 1	22,819	H	Middlesbrough	W 1 - 0	Crooks
30-Jan-82	Division 1	30,709	A	Everton	D 1 - 1	Villa
06-Feb-82	Division 1	29,960	H	Wolves	W 6 - 1	Villa(3), Falco, Hoddle (pen), Crooks
17-Feb-82	Division 1	23,877	A	Aston Villa	D 1 - 1	Crooks
20-Feb-82	Division 1	46,181	H	Manchester City	W 2 - 0	Hoddle (2, 1pen)
27-Feb-82	Division 1	20,592	A	Stoke City	W 2 - 0	Crooks (2)
09-Mar-82	Division 1	27,082	A	Brighton & HA	W 3 - 1	Ardiles, Archibald, Crooks
20-Mar-82	Division 1	46,827	H	Southampton	W 3 - 2	Roberts (3)
23-Mar-82	Division 1	17,708	A	Birmingham City	D 0 - 0	
27-Mar-82	Division 1	20,151	A	West Bromwich Albion	L 0 - 1	
29-Mar-82	Division 1	40,940	H	Arsenal	D 2 - 2	Hughton, Archibald
10-Apr-82	Division 1	45,215	H	Ipswich Town	W 1 - 0	Hoddle
12-Apr-82	Division 1	48,897	A	Arsenal	W 3 - 1	Hazard, Crooks (2)
14-Apr-82	Division 1	39,898	H	Sunderland	D 2 - 2	Galvin, Hoddle
17-Apr-82	Division 1	50,724	A	Manchester United	L 0 - 2	

24-Apr-82	Division 1	38,017	H	Notts County	W 3 - 1 Villa, Archibald, Galvin
28-Apr-82	Division 1	25,470	H	Birmingham City	D 1 - 1 Villa
01-May-82	Division 1	15,408	A	Coventry City	D 0 - 0
03-May-82	Division 1	38,091	H	Liverpool	D 2 - 2 Perryman, Archibald
05-May-82	Division 1	26,348	H	Swansea City	W 2 - 1 Brooke (2, 1pen)
08-May-82	Division 1	35,020	H	Leeds United	W 2 - 1 Brooke, Burns og
10-May-82	Division 1	27,667	A	West Ham United	D 2 - 2 Hoddle (pen), Brooke
12-May-82	Division 1	15,273	A	Nottingham Forest	L 0 - 2
15-May-82	Division 1	48,122	A	Liverpool	L 1 - 3 Hoddle
17-May-82	Division 1	21,202	A	Ipswich Town	L 1 - 2 Crooks

Tottenham Hotspur in the FA Cup - Season 1981-1982   WINNERS

02-Jan-82	F.A. Cup 3	38,421	H	Arsenal	W 1 - 0 Crooks
23-Jan-82	F.A. Cup 4	46,126	H	Leeds United	W 1 - 0 Crooks
13-Feb-82	F.A. Cup 5	43,419	H	Aston Villa	W 1 - 0 Falco
06-Mar-82	F.A. Cup 6	42,557	A	Chelsea	W 3 - 2 Hazard, Archibald, Hoddle
03-Apr-82	F.A. Cup SF	46,606	VP	Leicester City	W 2 - 0 Crooks, Wilson og.
22-May-82	F.A. Cup Final	100,000	W	Queens Park Rangers	D 1 - 1 Hoddle
27-May-82	F.A. Cup Final	92,000	W	Queens Park Rangers	W 1 - 0 Hoddle (pen)

Tottenham Hotspur in the League Cup - Season 1981-1982

Date	Round		Venue	Opponent	Result		Scorers
07-Oct-81	L.C. Cup 2 (1L)	39,333	H	Manchester United	W	1 - 0	Archibald
28-Oct-81	L.C. Cup 2 (2L)	55,890	A	Manchester United	W	1 - 0	Hazard
11-Nov-81	L.C. Cup 3	24,084	H	Wrexham	W	2 - 0	Hughton, Hoddle
02-Dec-81	L.C. Cup 4	30,214	H	Fulham	W	1 - 0	Hazard
18-Jan-82	L.C. Cup 5	31,192	H	Nottingham Forest	W	1 - 0	Ardiles
03-Feb-82	L.C. Cup SF (1)	32,238	A	West Bromwich Albion	D	0 - 0	
10-Feb-82	L.C. Cup SF (2)	47,241	H	West Bromwich Albion	W	1 - 0	Hazard
13-Mar-82	L.C. Cup Final	100,000	W	Liverpool	L	1 - 3	(a.e.t) Archibald

Runners up

Tottenham Hotspur In the European Cup Winners Cup - Season 1981-1982

Date	Round		Venue	Opponent	Result		Scorers
16-Sep-81	ECWC 1 (1L)	27,500	A	Ajax	W	3 - 1	Falco (2), Villa
27-Sep-81	ECWC 1 (2L)	34,606	H	Ajax	W	3 - 0	Galvin, Falco, Ardiles
21-Oct-81	ECWC 2 (1L)	17,000	A	Dundalk	D	1 - 1	Crooks
04-Nov-81	ECWC 2 (2L)	33,455	H	Dundalk	W	1 - 0	Crooks
03-Mar-82	ECWC QF (1L)	38,172	H	Eintracht Frankfurt	W	2 - 0	Miller, Hazard
17-Mar-82	ECWC QF (2L)	41,000	A	Eintracht Frankfurt	L	1 - 2	Hoddle
07-Apr-82	ECWC SF (1L)	41,555	H	Barcelona	D	1 - 1	Roberts
21-Apr-82	ECWC SF (2L)	80,000	A	Barcelona	L	0 - 1	

Tottenham Hotspur in the Charity Shield - Season 1981-1982   Joint Winners

| 22-Aug-81 | Charity Shield | 92,500 W Aston Villa | D | 2 - 2 | Falco (2) |

Tottenham Hotspur - Friendly Matches - Season 1981-1982

08-Aug-81	Friendly	-	A Glentoran	D	3 - 3	Ardiles, Hoddle (pen), Falco
10-Aug-81	Friendly	-	A Limerick	W	6 - 2	Archibald, Hoddle (4), Falco
12-Aug-81	Friendly	-	A Norwich City	D	2 - 2	Brooke, Falco
16-Aug-81	Friendly	-	A Aberdeen	W	1 - 0	Brooke (pen)
12-Oct-81	Friendly/Test		A Luton Town	D	2 - 2	Hoddle, Crooks

Paul Price Testimonial

14-Nov-81	Friendly	-	A Israel Select XI	W	3 - 2	Hazard (3, 1pen)
22-Dec-81	Friendly	-	A Plymouth Argyle	D	1 - 1	Hoddle
29-Dec-81	Friendly	-	A Sporting Lisbon	L	2 - 3	Roberts, Villa
02-Feb-82	Friendly	-	A Jersey Select XI	W	8 - 3	Hughton (pen), Hazard, Perryman, Falco (2), Gibson (2), Crooks

1982 - 1983 – Manager Keith Burkinshaw

Season 1982-1983	Played	Won	Drew	Lost	For	Agst.	Points
Division 1 - 4th	42	20	9	13	65	50	69
F.A. Cup	3	2	0	1	3	3	5th Rnd
League Cup	5	3	1	1	8	7	5th Rnd
European Cup Winners Cup	4	2	1	1	9	5	2nd Rnd
Charity Shield (Liverpool)	1	0	0	1	0	1	RunnersUp
Total - Season 1982-1983	55	27	11	17	85	66	4th

Tottenham Hotspur in the League - Season 1982-1983

28-Aug-82	Division 1	35,195	H	Luton Town	D 2 - 2 Hazard, Mabbutt
31-Aug-82	Division 1	23,224	A	Ipswich Town	W 2 - 1 Archibald, Crooks
04-Sep-82	Division 1	30,563	A	Everton	L 1 - 3 Archibald
08-Sep-82	Division 1	26,579	H	Southampton	W 6 - 0 Brooke (pen), Perryman, Galvin (2), Villa, Crooks
11-Sep-82	Division 1	32,483	H	Manchester City	L 1 - 2 Mabbutt
18-Sep-82	Division 1	21,137	A	Sunderland	W 1 - 0 Brooke
25-Sep-82	Division 1	30,662	H	Nottingham Forest	W 4 - 1 Mabbutt (2), Crooks (2)
02-Oct-82	Division 1	16,381	A	Swansea City	L 0 - 2
09-Oct-82	Division 1	25,188	H	Coventry City	W 4 - 0 Crooks, Brooke (3, 1pen)
16-Oct-82	Division 1	21,668	A	Norwich City	D 0 - 0
23-Oct-82	Division 1	26,183	H	Notts County	W 4 - 2 Brooke, Mabbutt, Crooks (2)

Date	Competition	Attendance	Venue	Opponent	Result	Scorers
30-Oct-82	Division 1	25,992	A	Aston Villa	L 0 - 4	
06-Nov-82	Division 1	42,634	H	Watford	L 0 - 1	
13-Nov-82	Division 1	47,869	A	Manchester United	L 0 - 1	
20-Nov-82	Division 1	41,960	H	West Ham United	W 2 - 1	Archibald (2)
27-Nov-82	Division 1	40,691	A	Liverpool	L 0 - 3	
04-Dec-82	Division 1	26,608	H	West Bromwich Albion	D 1 - 1	Wile og
11-Dec-82	Division 1	15,849	A	Stoke City	L 0 - 2	
18-Dec-82	Division 1	20,946	H	Birmingham City	W 2 - 1	Mabbutt (2)
27-Dec-82	Division 1	51,497	A	Arsenal	L 0 - 2	
28-Dec-82	Division 1	23,994	H	Brighton & HA	W 2 - 0	Villa, Hughton
01-Jan-83	Division 1	33,383	A	West Ham United	L 0 - 3	
03-Jan-83	Division 1	28,455	H	Everton	W 2 - 1	Gibson (2)
15-Jan-83	Division 1	21,231	A	Luton Town	D 1 - 1	Hoddle
22-Jan-83	Division 1	25,250	H	Sunderland	D 1 - 1	Gibson
05-Feb-83	Division 1	26,357	A	Manchester City	D 2 - 2	Gibson, Brooke (pen)
12-Feb-83	Division 1	24,632	H	Swansea City	W 1 - 0	
26-Feb-83	Division 1	23,342	H	Norwich City	D 0 - 0	Crooks
05-Mar-83	Division 1	11,841	A	Notts County	L 0 - 3	
12-Mar-83	Division 1	11,027	A	Coventry City	D 1 - 1	Miller
19-Mar-83	Division 1	27,373	A	Watford	W 1 - 0	Falco
23-Mar-83	Division 1	22,455	H	Aston Villa	W 2 - 0	Falco (2)
02-Apr-83	Division 1	20,341	A	Brighton & HA	L 1 - 2	Roberts

Date	Competition		Venue	Opponent	Result
04-Apr-83	Division 1	43,642	H	Arsenal	W 5 - 0 Hughton (2), Brazil, Falco (2)
09-Apr-83	Division 1	18,265	A	Nottingham Forest	D 2 - 2 Mabbutt, Brazil
16-Apr-83	Division 1	30,587	H	Ipswich Town	W 3 - 1 Mabbutt, Brazil (2)
23-Apr-83	Division 1	14,879	A	West Bromwich Albion	W 1 - 0 Archibald
30-Apr-83	Division 1	44,907	H	Liverpool	W 2 - 0 Archibald (2)
03-May-83	Division 1	21,602	A	Southampton	W 2 - 1 Mabbutt, Brazil
07-May-83	Division 1	18,947	A	Birmingham City	L 0 - 2
11-May-83	Division 1	32,803	H	Manchester United	W 2 - 0 Roberts, Archibald
14-May-83	Division 1	33,691	H	Stoke City	W 4 - 1 Brazil, Archibald (3)

Tottenham Hotspur in the FA Cup - Season 1982-1983

Date	Competition		Venue	Opponent	Result
08-Jan-83	F.A. Cup 3	38,040	A	Southampton	W 1 - 0 Hazard
29-Jan-83	F.A. Cup 4	38,208	H	West Bromwich Albion	W 2 - 1 Gibson, Crooks
19-Feb-83	F.A. Cup 5	42,995	A	Everton	L 0 - 2

Tottenham Hotspur in the League Cup - Season 1982-1983

Date	Competition		Venue	Opponent	Result
06-Oct-82	L.C. Cup 2 (1L)	20,416	H	Brighton & HA	D 1 - 1 Brooke (pen)
26-Oct-82	L.C. Cup 2 (2L)	20,755	A	Brighton & HA	W 1 - 0 Crooks
09-Nov-82	L.C. Cup 3	14,366	A	Gillingham	W 4 - 2 Archibald (2), Crooks (2)
01-Dec-82	L.C. Cup 4	27,861	H	Luton Town	W 1 - 0 Villa
19-Jan-83	L.C. Cup 5	30,771	H	Burnley	L 1 - 4 Gibson

Tottenham Hotspur in the European Cup Winners Cup - Season 1982-1983

15-Sep-82	ECWC 1 (1L)	12,000	A	Coleraine	W 3 - 0 Archibald, Crooks (2)
28-Sep-82	ECWC 1 (2L)	20,925	H	Coleraine	W 4 - 0 Crooks, Mabbutt, Brooke, Gibson
20-Oct-82	ECWC 2 (1L)	36,488	H	Bayern Munich	D 1 - 1 Archibald
03-Nov-82	ECWC 2 (2L)	50,000	A	Bayern Munich	L 1 - 4 Hughton

Tottenham Hotspur in the Charity Shield - Season 1982-1983   Runners up

21-Aug-82	Charity Shield	82,500	W	Liverpool	L 0 - 1

Tottenham Hotspur - Friendly Matches - Season 1982-1983

Date		Opponent	Result	Scorers
03-Aug-82 Friendly	- A	Scunthorpe United	W 5 - 0	Falco (2), Gibson (2), Roberts
06-Aug-82 Friendly	- A	FC Lausanne	L 0 - 3	
08-Aug-82 Friendly	- A	Glasgow Rangers	W 1 - 0	Mabbutt
20-Sep-82 Friendly	- A	Barnet	L 1 - 2	Hazard
20-Dec-82 Friendly	- N	Borussia Moechengladbach	L 0 - 2	
22-Dec-82 Friendly	- A	Israel Select XI	D 2 - 2	Brooke, Mazzon
26-Mar-83 Friendly	- A	Northerners Guernsey	W 6 - 1	Hazard, Archibald (3), Brazil (2)
19-Apr-83 Friendly	- A	Bristol Rovers	W 3 - 2	O'Reilly, Perryman, Crooks
17-May-83 Friendly	- A	Trinidad & Tobago XI	D 2 - 2	Archibald, Crooks
20-May-83 Friendly	- A	ASL Trinidad	W 2 - 1	Gibson, Brazil
23-May-83 Friendly	- A	Charlton Athletic	D 4 - 4	Falco (4)
30-May-83 Friendly	- A	Aalesund Norway	W 3 - 2	Crooks (3)

213

Tottenham Hotspur Tour - Holland - Amsterdam 707 Tournament - August 1982

13-Aug-82 Tour/707T-1   - A **Ajax**   L   2 - 3 Roberts (2)
15-Aug-82 Tour/707T-3/4 - A **1FC Cologne**   D   0 - 0

Spurs lost the third/fourth place match 1-3 on penalties (scorer: Archibald)

Tottenham Hotspur Tour - Swaziland - Royal Swazi Hotel Tournament – June1983

04-Jun-83 Tour/RSHT   - A **Manchester United**   L   1 - 2 Archibald
11-Jun-83 Tour/RSHT   - A **Manchester United**   W   2 - 0 Perryman, Mabbutt

Spurs won the Tournament 3-2 on penalties (Scorers: Brazil, Price, Perryman)

214

1983 - 1984 – Manager Keith Burkinshaw

Season 1983-1984	Played	Won	Drew	Lost	For	Agst.	Points
Division 1 - 8th	42	17	10	15	64	65	61
F.A. Cup	4	1	2	1	2	2	4th Rnd
League Cup	3	1	0	2	5	5	3rd Rnd
UEFA Cup – Winners	12	7	3	2	30	9	Winners
Total - Season 1983-1984	61	26	15	20	101	81	8th

Tottenham Hotspur in the League - Season 1983-1984

27-Aug-83	Division 1	26,562	A	Ipswich Town	L	1 - 3	Archibald
29-Aug-83	Division 1	35,434	H	Coventry City	D	1 - 1	Hoddle (pen)
03-Sep-83	Division 1	38,042	H	West Ham United	L	0 - 2	
07-Sep-83	Division 1	14,830	A	West Bromwich Albion	D	1 - 1	Roberts
10-Sep-83	Division 1	15,886	A	Leicester City	W	3 - 0	Stevens, Mabbutt, Crooks
17-Sep-83	Division 1	29,125	H	Everton	L	1 - 2	Falco
24-Sep-83	Division 1	21,056	A	Watford	W	3 - 2	Hughton, Hoddle, Archibald
02-Oct-83	Division 1	30,596	H	Nottingham Forest	W	2 - 1	Stevens, Archibald
15-Oct-83	Division 1	12,523	A	Wolves	W	3 - 2	Archibald (2), Falco
22-Oct-83	Division 1	18,937	A	Birmingham City	W	1 - 0	Archibald
29-Oct-83	Division 1	29,198	H	Notts County	W	1 - 0	Archibald
05-Nov-83	Division 1	14,726	A	Stoke City	D	1 - 1	Falco

Date	Competition	Attendance	Venue	Opponent	Result	Score	Scorers
12-Nov-83	Division 1	44,348	H	Liverpool	D	2 - 2	Archibald, Hoddle (pen)
19-Nov-83	Division 1	17,275	A	Luton Town	W	4 - 2	Dick, Archibald (2), Cooke
26-Nov-83	Division 1	39,789	H	Queens Park Rangers	W	3 - 2	Archibald, Falco (2)
03-Dec-83	Division 1	21,987	A	Norwich City	L	1 - 2	Dick
10-Dec-83	Division 1	29,711	H	Southampton	D	0 - 0	
16-Dec-83	Division 1	33,616	A	Manchester United	L	2 - 4	Brazil, Falco
26-Dec-83	Division 1	38,756	H	Arsenal	L	2 - 4	Roberts, Archibald
27-Dec-83	Division 1	30,125	A	Aston Villa	D	0 - 0	
31-Dec-83	Division 1	30,939	A	West Ham United	L	1 - 4	Stevens
02-Jan-84	Division 1	32,495	H	Watford	L	2 - 3	Hughton, Hoddle (pen)
14-Jan-84	Division 1	25,832	H	Ipswich Town	W	2 - 0	Roberts, Falco
21-Jan-84	Division 1	17,990	A	Everton	L	1 - 2	Archibald
04-Feb-84	Division 1	21,482	A	Nottingham Forest	D	2 - 2	Hughton, Falco
08-Feb-84	Division 1	19,327	H	Sunderland	W	3 - 0	Perryman, Archibald (2)
11-Feb-84	Division 1	29,410	H	Leicester City	W	3 - 2	Archibald, Falco, Galvin
21-Feb-84	Division 1	7,943	A	Notts County	D	0 - 0	
25-Feb-84	Division 1	23,564	H	Birmingham City	L	0 - 1	
03-Mar-84	Division 1	18,271	H	Stoke City	W	1 - 0	Falco (pen)
10-Mar-84	Division 1	36,718	A	Liverpool	L	1 - 3	Stevens
17-Mar-84	Division 1	22,385	H	West Bromwich Albion	L	0 - 1	
24-Mar-84	Division 1	12,847	A	Coventry City	W	4 - 2	Roberts, Hazard, Brazil (2, 1pen)
31-Mar-84	Division 1	19,296	H	Wolves	W	1 - 0	Hazard

Date	Competition	Att.		Opponent	Result			Scorers
07-Apr-84	Division 1	15,433	A	Sunderland	D	1 - 1		Falco
14-Apr-84	Division 1	25,390	H	Luton Town	W	2 - 1		Roberts, Falco
18-Apr-84	Division 1	18,668	H	Aston Villa	W	2 - 1		Roberts (pen), Mabbutt
21-Apr-84	Division 1	48,931	A	Arsenal	L	2 - 3		Archibald (2)
28-Apr-84	Division 1	24,937	A	Queens Park Rangers	L	1 - 2		Archibald
05-May-84	Division 1	18,874	H	Norwich City	W	2 - 0		Archibald, Falco
07-May-84	Division 1	21,141	A	Southampton	L	0 - 5		
12-May-84	Division 1	39,790	H	Manchester United	D	1 - 1		Archibald

Tottenham Hotspur in the FA Cup - Season 1983-1984

Date	Competition	Att.		Opponent	Result			Scorers
07-Jan-84	F.A. Cup 3	23,398	A	Fulham	D	0 - 0		
11-Jan-84	F.A. Cup 3	32,898	H	Fulham	W	2 - 0		Roberts, Archibald
28-Jan-84	F.A. Cup 4	37,792	H	Norwich City	D	0 - 0		
01-Feb-84	F.A. Cup 4	26,811	A	Norwich City	L	1 - 2		Falco

Tottenham Hotspur in the League Cup - Season 1983-1984

Date	Competition	Att.		Opponent	Result			Scorers
05-Oct-83	L.C. Cup 2 (1L)	20,491	H	Lincoln City	W	3 - 1		Galvin, Archibald, Houghton og
26-Oct-83	L.C. Cup 2 (2L)	12,239	A	Lincoln City	L	1 - 2		Falco
09-Nov-83	L.C. Cup 3	48,200	H	Arsenal	L	1 - 2		Hoddle (pen)

Tottenham Hotspur in the UEFA Cup – Season 1983-1984   WINNERS

Date	Competition		Venue	Result			Scorers
14-Sep-83	UEFA 1 (1L)	7,000	A	Drogheda United	W	6 - 0	Falco (2), Crooks, Galvin, Mabbutt (2)
28-Sep-83	UEFA 1 (2L)	19,891	H	Drogheda United	W	8 - 0	Falco (2),Roberts (2),Brazil (2),Archibald, Hughton
19-Oct-83	UEFA 2 (1L)	35,404	H	Feyenoord	W	4 - 2	Archibald (2), Galvin (2)
02-Nov-83	UEFA 2 (2L)	45,061	A	Feyenoord	W	2 - 0	Hughton, Galvin
23-Nov-83	UEFA 3(1L)	20,000	A	Bayern Munich	L	0 - 1	
07-Dec-83	UEFA 3 (2L)	41,977	H	Bayern Munich	W	2 - 0	Archibald, Falco
07-Mar-84	UEFA 4 (1L)	34,069	H	Austria Vienna	W	2 - 0	Archibald, Brazil
21-Mar-84	UEFA 4 (2L)	31,000	A	Austria Vienna	D	2 - 2	Brazil, Ardiles
11-Apr-84	UEFA SF (1L)	40,000	A	Hajduk Split	L	1 - 2	Falco
25-Apr-84	UEFA SF (2L)	43,969	H	Hajduk Split	W	1 - 0	Hazard (Spurs win on away goals)
09-May-84	UEFA Final (1L)	40,000	A	Anderlecht	D	1 - 1	Miller
25-May-84	UEFA Final (2L)	46,205	H	Anderlecht	D	1 - 1	Roberts

Tottenham Hotspur win the UEFA cup 4-3 on penalties after 2-2 on aggregate
Penalty takers (Roberts [scored], Falco [scored], Stevens [scored], Archibald [scored], Thomas [saved])

Tottenham Hotspur - Friendly Matches - Season 1983-1984

Date			Opponent	Result			Scorers
02-Aug-83	Friendly	- A	Hertford Town	W	2 - 1	Archibald, Crooks
04-Aug-83	Friendly	- A	Enfield	W	4 - 1	Roberts, Hoddle, Crooks (2)
06-Aug-83	Friendly	- A	Brentford	W	4 - 2	Roberts, Brazil, Crooks,Whitehead og
09-Aug-83	Friendly	- A	Portsmouth	W	3 - 1	Roberts, Galvin, Mabbutt

218

12-Aug-83	Friendly	- A	Brighton & HA	D	0 - 0	
16-Aug-83	Friendly	- A	Glasgow Celtic	D	1 - 1	Falco
17-Aug-83	Friendly	- A	Dundee United	D	1 - 1	Galvin
21-Aug-83	Friendly/Test	H	West Ham United	D	1 - 1	Brazil

Bill Nicholson Testimonial

08-Oct-83	Friendly	- A	Vale Recreation	W	7 - 2	Hazard, Archibald (4), Brazil, Falco
26-Mar-84	Friendly	- A	Wimbledon	W	5 - 0	Hazard, Falco (2), Crooks (2)
18-May-84	Friendly	- A	West Ham United	L	1 - 4	Archibald
29-May-84	Friendly/Test	H	England XI	D	2 - 2	Hughton, Brady

Keith Burkinshaw Testimonial

Tottenham Hotspur Tour – Swaziland - RoyalSwaziHotel Tournament – June1984

| 02-Jun-84 | Tour/RSSC | - A | Liverpool | L | 2 - 5 | Thomas, Falco |
| 09-Jun-84 | Tour/RSSC | - A | Liverpool | D | 1 - 1 | Brazil |

219

1984 - 1985 – Manager Peter Shreeves

Season 1984-1985	Played	Won	Drew	Lost	For	Agst.	Points
Division 1 - 3rd	42	23	8	11	78	51	77
F.A. Cup	3	1	1	1	3	3	4th Rnd
League Cup	5	3	1	1	11	3	4th Rnd
UEFA Cup	8	4	2	2	16	4	4th Rnd
Total - Season 1984-1985	58	31	12	15	108	61	3rd

Tottenham Hotspur in the League - Season 1984-1985

25-Aug-84	Division 1	A	Everton	35,630	W	4 - 1	Falco, Allen C (2), Chiedozie
27-Aug-84	Division 1	H	Leicester City	30,046	D	2 - 2	Roberts (2, 1pen)
01-Sep-84	Division 1	H	Norwich City	24,947	W	3 - 1	Chiedozie, Falco, Galvin
04-Sep-84	Division 1	A	Sunderland	18,895	L	0 - 1	
08-Sep-84	Division 1	A	Sheffield Wednesday	33,421	L	1 - 2	Falco
15-Sep-84	Division 1	H	Queens Park Rangers	31,655	W	5 - 0	Falco (2), Allen C (2), Hazard
22-Sep-84	Division 1	A	Aston Villa	22,409	W	1 - 0	Chiedozie
29-Sep-84	Division 1	H	Luton Town	30,204	W	4 - 2	Roberts (pen), Perryman, Falco, Hazard
06-Oct-84	Division 1	A	Southampton	21,825	L	0 - 1	
12-Oct-84	Division 1	H	Liverpool	28,599	W	1 - 0	Crooks
20-Oct-84	Division 1	A	Manchester United	54,516	L	0 - 1	
27-Oct-84	Division 1	H	Stoke City	23,477	W	4 - 0	Roberts (pen), Chiedozie, Allen C (2)

220

Date	Competition	Venue	Opponent	Attendance	Result	Score	Scorers
03-Nov-84	Division 1	H	West Bromwich Albion	24,494	L	2 - 3	Chiedozie, Hazard
10-Nov-84	Division 1	A	Nottingham Forest	21,306	W	2 - 1	Hazard, Galvin
17-Nov-84	Division 1	A	Ipswich Town	21,894	W	3 - 0	Mabbutt, Allen C, Hoddle
24-Nov-84	Division 1	H	Chelsea	31,197	D	1 - 1	Falco
01-Dec-84	Division 1	A	Coventry City	14,518	D	1 - 1	Falco
08-Dec-84	Division 1	H	Newcastle United	29,695	W	3 - 1	Roberts (pen), Falco (2)
15-Dec-84	Division 1	A	Watford	24,225	W	2 - 1	Falco, Crooks
22-Dec-84	Division 1	A	Norwich City	17,682	W	2 - 1	Galvin, Crooks
26-Dec-84	Division 1	H	West Ham United	37,186	D	2 - 2	Mabbutt, Crooks
29-Dec-84	Division 1	H	Sunderland	26,930	W	2 - 0	Hoddle, Crooks
01-Jan-85	Division 1	A	Arsenal	48,714	W	2 - 1	Falco, Crooks
12-Jan-85	Division 1	A	Queens Park Rangers	27,404	D	2 - 2	Falco, Crooks
02-Feb-85	Division 1	A	Luton Town	17,511	D	2 - 2	Roberts, Falco
23-Feb-85	Division 1	A	West Bromwich Albion	15,418	W	1 - 0	Falco
02-Mar-85	Division 1	A	Stoke City	12,552	W	1 - 0	Crooks
12-Mar-85	Division 1	H	Manchester United	42,918	L	1 - 2	Falco
16-Mar-85	Division 1	A	Liverpool	43,852	W	1 - 0	Crooks
23-Mar-85	Division 1	H	Southampton	33,772	W	5 - 1	Ardiles, Falco, Hoddle, Crooks, Brooke
30-Mar-85	Division 1	H	Aston Villa	27,971	L	0 - 2	
03-Apr-85	Division 1	H	Everton	48,108	L	1 - 2	Roberts
06-Apr-85	Division 1	A	West Ham United	24,435	D	1 - 1	Ardiles
13-Apr-85	Division 1	A	Leicester City	15,609	W	2 - 1	Falco, Hoddle

17-Apr-85	Division 1		40,399	H	Arsenal	L	0 - 2	
20-Apr-85	Division 1		20,348	H	Ipswich Town	L	2 - 3	Leworthy (2)
27-Apr-85	Division 1		26,310	A	Chelsea	D	1 - 1	Galvin
04-May-85	Division 1		16,711	H	Coventry City	W	4 - 2	Falco (2), Hoddle, Hughton
06-May-85	Division 1		29,702	A	Newcastle United	W	3 - 2	Leworthy, Hoddle, Crook
11-May-85	Division 1		23,167	H	Watford	L	1 - 5	Hoddle (pen)
14-May-85	Division 1		15,669	H	Sheffield Wednesday	W	2 - 0	Falco, Hoddle (pen)
17-May-85	Division 1		20,075	H	Nottingham Forest	W	1 - 0	Falco

Tottenham Hotspur in the FA Cup - Season 1984-1985

05-Jan-85	F.A. Cup 3		29,029	H	Charlton Athletic	D	1 - 1	Crooks
23-Jan-85	F.A. Cup 3		21,406	A	Charlton Athletic	W	2 - 1	Falco, Galvin
27-Jan-85	F.A. Cup 4		27,905	A	Liverpool	L	0 - 1	

Tottenham Hotspur in the League Cup - Season 1984-1985

26-Sep-84	L.C. Cup 2 (1L)	7,027	A	Halifax Town	W	5 - 1	Falco (2), Crooks (3)
09-Oct-84	L.C. Cup 2 (2L)	14,802	H	Halifax Town	W	4 - 0	Hughton, Hazard (2), Crooks
31-Oct-84	L.C. Cup 3	38,690	H	Liverpool	W	1 - 0	Allen C
21-Nov-84	L.C. Cup 4	27,421	A	Sunderland	D	0 - 0	
05-Dec-84	L.C. Cup 4	25,835	H	Sunderland	L	1 - 2	Roberts (pen)

Tottenham Hotspur in the UEFA Cup - Season 1984-1985

Date	Round		Venue	Opponent	Result		Score		Scorers
19-Sep-84	UEFA Cup 1 (1)	26,000	A	Sporting Braga	W	3 - 0	Falco (2), Galvin
03-Oct-84	UEFA Cup 1 (2)	22,478	H	Sporting Braga	W	6 - 0	Stevens, Hughton, Crooks (3), Falco
24-Oct-84	UEFA Cup 2 (1)	27,000	A	FC Bruges	L	1 - 2	Allen C
07-Nov-84	UEFA Cup 2 (2)	34,356	H	FC Bruges	W	3 - 0	Hazard, Allen C, Roberts
28-Nov-84	UEFA Cup 3(1)	27,971	H	Bohemians Prague	W	2 - 0	Ondra og, Stevens
12-Dec-84	UEFA Cup 3 (2)	17,500	A	Bohemians Prague	D	1 - 1	Falco
06-Mar-85	UEFA Cup 4 (1)	39,914	H	Real Madrid	L	0 - 1	
20-Mar-85	UEFA Cup 4 (2)	90,000	A	Real Madrid	D	0 - 0	

Tottenham Hotspur - Friendly Matches - Season 1984-1985

Date	Type		Venue	Opponent	Result	Score	Scorers
04-Aug-84	Friendly	-	A	Enfield	W	7 - 0	Stevens, Brooke, Hazard, Crooks (4)
06-Aug-84	Friendly	-	A	Nice	D	2 - 2	Miller (2)
11-Aug-84	Friendly	-	A	Brentford	W	3 - 0	Allen C (2), Galvin
16-Aug-84	Friendly	-	A	Manchester City	W	2 - 0	Roberts (pen), Galvin
18-Aug-84	Friendly	-	A	Sheffield United	W	3 - 0	Allen C (2), Falco
20-Aug-84	Friendly/Test	-	H	Fulham	W	3 - 1	Crooks, Allen C (2)

Peter Southey Memorial Match

Date	Type		Venue	Opponent	Result	Score	Scorers
12-Sep-84	Friendly	-	A	Real Madrid	L	0 - 1	
14-Oct-84	Friendly	-	A	Malta National XI	W	1 - 0	Dick
13-Nov-84	Friendly	-	A	Sutton United	W	5 - 3	Crooks (3), Crook, Falco
08-Mar-85	Friendly	-	N	Kuwait National XI	W	1 - 0	Crooks
08-Apr-85	Friendly	-	A	Guernsey FA XI	W	5 - 0	Clemence (pen), Falco (2), Crooks, Ardiles
29-Apr-85	Friendly	-	A	Bristol Rovers	W	6 - 2	Cooke, Leworthy (3), Dick (2)
08-May-85	Friendly/Test	-	A	Arsenal	W	3 - 2	Crook, Falco (2)

Pat Jennings Testimonial

Tottenham Hotspur Tour - Sweden & Norway - July 1984

Date	Type		Venue	Opponent	Result	Score	Scorers
27-Jul-84	Tour	-	A	Stjoerdals Blink	W	9 - 0	Kempes (3), Falco, Galvin, Ardiles, Hoddle, Crooks, og
29-Jul-84	Tour	-	A	Ostersund	W	4 - 0	Galvin, Stevens, Crooks, Hoddle (pen)
30-Jul-84	Tour	-	A	Viking	W	1 - 0	Crooks

Tottenham Hotspur Tour - Hong Kong - May 1985

23-May-85	Tour	-	A Seiko FC	W	4 - 0	Mabbutt (2), Falco, Dick

Tottenham Hotspur Tour - Australia - $200,000 Tournament – June 1985

29-May-85	Tour/$200T	-	A Australia Federation	L	0 - 1	
01-Jun-85	Tour/$200T	-	A Udinese	L	0 - 2	
05-Jun-85	Tour/$200T	-	A Vasco da Gama	D	1 - 1	Falco

1985 – 1986 – Manager Peter Shreeves

Season 1985-1986	Played	Won	Drew	Lost	For	Agst.	Points
Division 1 – 10th	42	19	8	15	74	52	65
F.A. Cup	5	2	2	1	10	5	5th Rnd
League Cup	6	2	2	2	6	3	4th Rnd
Screen Sport Super Cup	6	2	1	3	6	9	SemiFinal
Total - Season 1985-1986	59	25	13	21	96	69	10th

Tottenham Hotspur in the League - Season 1985-1986

17-Aug-85 Division 1	29,884 H Watford	W 4 - 0 Allen P, Falco, Waddle (2)
21-Aug-85 Division 1	10,634 A Oxford United	D 1 - 1 Thomas D
24-Aug-85 Division 1	17,758 A Ipswich Town	L 0 - 1
26-Aug-85 Division 1	29,750 H Everton	L 0 - 1
31-Aug-85 Division 1	27,789 A Manchester City	L 1 - 2 Miller
04-Sep-85 Division 1	23,642 H Chelsea	W 4 - 1 Roberts, Miller, Falco, Chiedozie
07-Sep-85 Division 1	23,883 H Newcastle United	W 5 - 1 Falco, Chiedozie (2), Hoddle, Hazard
14-Sep-85 Division 1	17,554 A Nottingham Forest	W 1 - 0 Hughton
21-Sep-85 Division 1	23,601 H Sheffield Wednesday	W 5 - 1 Falco (2), Hoddle, Waddle (2)
28-Sep-85 Division 1	41,521 A Liverpool	L 1 - 4 Chiedozie
05-Oct-85 Division 1	12,040 A West Bromwich Albion	D 1 - 1 Waddle
19-Oct-85 Division 1	13,545 A Coventry City	W 3 - 2 Falco, Hoddle (pen) Chiedozie

226

Date	Competition	Attendance	H/A	Opponent	Result	Scorers
26-Oct-85	Division 1	17,944	H	Leicester City	L 1 - 3	Falco
02-Nov-85	Division 1	17,440	A	Southampton	L 0 - 1	
09-Nov-85	Division 1	19,163	H	Luton Town	L 1 - 3	Cooke
16-Nov-85	Division 1	54,575	A	Manchester United	D 0 - 0	
23-Nov-85	Division 1	20,334	H	Queens Park Rangers	D 1 - 1	Mabbutt
30-Nov-85	Division 1	14,099	A	Aston Villa	W 2 - 1	Mabbutt, Falco
07-Dec-85	Division 1	17,698	H	Oxford United	W 5 - 1	Falco, Allen C (2), Hoddle, Waddle
14-Dec-85	Division 1	16,327	A	Watford	L 0 - 1	
21-Dec-85	Division 1	18,845	H	Ipswich Town	W 2 - 0	Allen C, Hoddle
26-Dec-85	Division 1	33,835	H	West Ham United	W 1 - 0	Perryman
28-Dec-85	Division 1	37,115	A	Chelsea	L 0 - 2	
01-Jan-86	Division 1	45,109	A	Arsenal	D 0 - 0	
11-Jan-86	Division 1	19,043	H	Nottingham Forest	L 0 - 3	
18-Jan-86	Division 1	17,009	H	Manchester City	L 0 - 2	
01-Feb-86	Division 1	33,178	A	Everton	L 0 - 1	
08-Feb-86	Division 1	13,135	H	Coventry City	L 0 - 1	
22-Feb-86	Division 1	23,232	A	Sheffield Wednesday	W 2 - 1	Chiedozie, Howells
02-Mar-86	Division 1	16,436	H	Liverpool	L 1 - 2	Waddle
08-Mar-86	Division 1	10,841	H	West Bromwich Albion	W 5 - 0	Mabbutt, Falco (2), Galvin, Waddle
15-Mar-86	Division 1	9,394	A	Birmingham City	W 2 - 1	Stevens, Waddle
22-Mar-86	Division 1	30,645	A	Newcastle United	D 2 - 2	Hoddle, Waddle
29-Mar-86	Division 1	33,427	H	Arsenal	W 1 - 0	Stevens

227

Date		Venue	Opponent	Attendance	Result	Scorers
31-Mar-86	Division 1	A	West Ham United	27,497	L	1 - 2	Ardiles
05-Apr-86	Division 1	A	Leicester City	9,574	W	4 - 1	Bowen, Falco (3)
12-Apr-86	Division 1	A	Luton Town	13,141	D	1 - 1	Allen C
16-Apr-86	Division 1	H	Birmingham City	9,359	W	2 - 0	Chiedozie, Falco
19-Apr-86	Division 1	H	Manchester United	32,357	D	0 - 0	
26-Apr-86	Division 1	A	Queens Park Rangers	17,768	W	5 - 2	Falco (2), Allen C (2), Hoddle
03-May-86	Division 1	H	Aston Villa	14,854	W	4 - 2	Falco (2), Allen C (2)
05-May-86	Division 1	H	Southampton	13,036	W	5 - 3	Galvin (3), Allen C, Waddle

Tottenham Hotspur in the FA Cup - Season 1985-1986

04-Jan-86	F.A. Cup 3	10,638	A	Oxford United	D 1 - 1 Chiedozie
08-Jan-86	F.A. Cup 3	19,136	H	Oxford United	W 2 - 1 (a.e.t) Waddle, Allen C
25-Jan-86	F.A. Cup 4	17,546	A	Notts County	D 1 - 1 Allen C
29-Jan-86	F.A. Cup 4	17,393	H	Notts County	W 5 - 0 Chiedozie, Falco, Allen C, Hoddle, Waddle
04-Mar-86	F.A. Cup 5	23,338	H	Everton	L 1 - 2 Falco

Tottenham Hotspur in the League Cup - Season 1985-1986

23-Sep-85	L.C. Cup 2 (1L)	13,828	A	Orient	L 0 - 2
30-Oct-85	L.C. Cup 2 (2L)	21,046	H	Orient	W 4 - 0 Roberts (2), Galvin, Waddle
06-Nov-85	L.C. Cup 3	16,899	H	Wimbledon	W 2 - 0 Leworthy, Mabbutt
20-Nov-85	L.C. Cup 4	28,619	H	Portsmouth	D 0 - 0
27-Nov-85	L.C. Cup 4	28,100	A	Portsmouth	D 0 - 0
10-Dec-85	L.C. Cup 4	26,306	A	Portsmouth	L 0 - 1

Tottenham Hotspur in the Screen Sport Super Cup - Season 1985-1986

02-Oct-85	SSS Cup Gp.	11,549	H	Southampton	W 2 - 1 Falco (2)
03-Dec-85	SSS Cup Gp.	14,855	A	Liverpool	L 0 - 2
17-Dec-85	SSS Cup Gp.	4,680	A	Southampton	W 3 - 1 Falco, Allen C, Leworthy
14-Jan-86	SSS Cup Gp.	10,078	H	Liverpool	L 0 - 2
05-Feb-86	SSS Cup SF 1	7,548	H	Everton	D 0 - 0
19-Mar-86	SSS Cup SF 2	12,008	A	Everton	L 1 - 3 (a.e.t) Falco

229

Tottenham Hotspur - Friendly Matches - Season 1985-1986

Date			Opponent	Result	Scorers
18-Jul-85	Friendly	- A	Wycombe Wanderers	W 4 - 1	Thomas, Leworthy, Waddle, Galvin
24-Jul-85	Friendly	- A	Chesterfield	W 4 - 2	Roberts, Waddle (2), Chiedozie
27-Jul-85	Friendly	- A	AFC Bournemouth	W 3 - 0	Miller, Falco, Galvin
31-Jul-85	Friendly	- A	Plymouth Argyle	L 0 - 1	
03-Aug-85	Friendly	- A	Exeter City	D 2 - 2	Falco, Hazard
04-Aug-85	Friendly/Test	H	Arsenal	D 1 - 1	Leworthy

Glenn Hoddle Testimonial

Date			Opponent	Result	Scorers
10-Aug-85	Friendly	- A	Norwich City	D 1 - 1	Leworthy
10-Sep-85	Friendly	- A	Fareham Town	W 6 - 3	Chiedozie, Leworthy (3), Cooke, Samways
14-Oct-85	Friendly	- A	Maidstone United	W 2 - 1	Falco, Galvin
10-Feb-86	Friendly	- A	Jersey Select XI	W 7 - 0	Allen C (2, 1pen), Thomas, Waddle, Hoddle, Allen P, Mabbutt
06-Apr-86	Friendly	- A	Glasgow Rangers	W 2 - 0	Chiedozie, Allen P
22-Apr-86	Friendly	- A	Chelmsford City	W 8 - 2	Falco (5), Allen C (2), Chiedozie
01-May-86	Friendly/Test	H	Inter Milan	W 2 - 1	Falco, Allen C

Osvaldo Ardiles Benefit Match

Date			Opponent	Result	Scorers
09-May-86	Friendly	- A	Brentford	L 3 - 4	Chiedozie, Allen C (2)
12-May-86	Friendly	- A	West Ham United	L 1 - 5	Allen C

230

1986 – 1987 – Manager David Pleat

Season 1986-1987	Played	Won	Drew	Lost	For	Agst.	Points
Division 1 - 3rd	42	21	8	13	68	43	71
F.A. Cup - Runners Up	6	5	0	1	16	6	RunnersUp
League Cup	9	6	1	2	25	11	SemiFinal
Total - Season 1986-1987	57	32	9	16	109	60	3rd

Tottenham Hotspur in the League - Season 1986-1987

23-Aug-86	Division 1	24,712	A	Aston Villa	W 3 - 0 Allen C (3)
25-Aug-86	Division 1	25,381	H	Newcastle United	D 1 - 1 Allen C
30-Aug-86	Division 1	23,164	H	Manchester City	W 1 - 0 Roberts
02-Sep-86	Division 1	17,911	A	Southampton	L 0 - 2
06-Sep-86	Division 1	44,703	A	Arsenal	D 0 - 0
13-Sep-86	Division 1	28,202	H	Chelsea	L 1 - 3 Allen C (pen)
20-Sep-86	Division 1	13,141	A	Leicester City	W 2 - 1 Allen C (2)
27-Sep-86	Division 1	28,007	H	Everton	W 2 - 0 Allen C (2)
04-Oct-86	Division 1	22,738	H	Luton Town	D 0 - 0
11-Oct-86	Division 1	43,139	A	Liverpool	W 1 - 0 Allen C
18-Oct-86	Division 1	26,876	H	Sheffield Wednesday	D 1 - 1 Allen C
25-Oct-86	Division 1	18,579	A	Queens Park Rangers	L 0 - 2
01-Nov-86	Division 1	21,820	H	Wimbledon	L 1 - 2 Thomas M

Date		Att.		Venue / Opponent	Result	Scorers
08-Nov-86	Division 1	22,019	A	Norwich City	L 1 - 2	Claesen
15-Nov-86	Division 1	20,255	H	Coventry City	W 1 - 0	Allen C
22-Nov-86	Division 1	12,143	A	Oxford United	W 4 - 2	Allen C (2), Waddle (2)
29-Nov-86	Division 1	30,042	H	Nottingham Forest	L 2 - 3	Allen C (2)
07-Dec-86	Division 1	35,267	A	Manchester United	D 3 - 3	Mabbutt, Allen C, Moran og
13-Dec-86	Division 1	23,137	H	Watford	W 2 - 1	Gough, Hoddle
20-Dec-86	Division 1	21,576	A	Chelsea	W 2 - 0	Allen C (2)
26-Dec-86	Division 1	39,019	H	West Ham United	W 4 - 0	Hodge, Allen C (2), Waddle
27-Dec-86	Division 1	22,175	A	Coventry City	L 3 - 4	Allen C (2), Claesen
01-Jan-87	Division 1	19,744	A	Charlton Athletic	W 2 - 0	Claesen, Galvin
04-Jan-87	Division 1	37,723	H	Arsenal	L 1 - 2	Thomas M
24-Jan-87	Division 1	19,121	H	Aston Villa	W 3 - 0	Hodge (2), Claesen
14-Feb-87	Division 1	22,066	H	Southampton	W 2 - 0	Hodge, Gough
25-Feb-87	Division 1	16,038	H	Leicester City	W 5 - 0	Allen C (2, 1pen), Allen P, Claesen
07-Mar-87	Division 1	21,071	H	Queens Park Rangers	W 1 - 0	Allen C (pen)
22-Mar-87	Division 1	32,763	H	Liverpool	W 1 - 0	Waddle
25-Mar-87	Division 1	30,836	A	Newcastle United	D 1 - 1	Hoddle
28-Mar-87	Division 1	13,447	A	Luton Town	L 1 - 3	Waddle
04-Apr-87	Division 1	22,400	H	Norwich City	W 3 - 0	Allen C (3)
07-Apr-87	Division 1	19,488	A	Sheffield Wednesday	W 1 - 0	Allen C
15-Apr-87	Division 1	21,460	A	Manchester City	D 1 - 1	Claesen
18-Apr-87	Division 1	26,926	H	Charlton Athletic	W 1 - 0	Allen C

20-Apr-87	Division 1	23,972	A	West Ham United	L	1 - 2	Allen C
22-Apr-87	Division 1	7,917	A	Wimbledon	D	2 - 2	Claesen, Bowen
25-Apr-87	Division 1	20,064	H	Oxford United	W	3 - 1	Allen P, Waddle, Hoddle
02-May-87	Division 1	19,837	A	Nottingham Forest	L	0 - 2	
04-May-87	Division 1	36,692	H	Manchester United	W	4 - 0	Thomas M (2), Allen C (pen), Allen P
09-May-87	Division 1	20,024	A	Watford	L	0 - 1	
11-May-87	Division 1	28,287	A	Everton	L	0 - 1	

Tottenham Hotspur in the FA Cup - Season 1986-1987   Runners up

10-Jan-87	F.A. Cup 3	19,339	H	Scunthorpe United	W 3 - 2 Mabbutt, Waddle, Claesen
31-Jan-87	F.A. Cup 4	29,603	H	Crystal Palace	W 4 - 0 Mabbutt, Allen C (pen), Claesen, O'Reilly og
21-Feb-87	F.A. Cup 5	38,033	H	Newcastle United	W 1 - 0 Allen C (pen)
15-Mar-87	F.A. Cup 6	15,636	A	Wimbledon	W 2 - 0 Waddle, Hoddle
11-Apr-87	F.A. Cup SF	46,151	VP	Watford	W 4 - 1 Hodge (2), Allen C, Allen P
16-May-87	F.A. Cup Final	98,000	W	Coventry City	L 2 - 3 Allen C, Mabbutt

Tottenham Hotspur in the League Cup - Season 1986-1987

23-Sep-86	L.C. Cup 2 (1L)	10,079	A	Barnsley	W 3 - 2 Roberts, Allen C, Waddle
08-Oct-86	L.C. Cup 2 (2L)	12,299	H	Barnsley	W 5 - 3 Close, Hoddle (2), Galvin, Allen C
29-Oct-86	L.C. Cup 3	15,542	H	Birmingham City	W 5 - 0 Roberts, Allen C (2), Hoddle, Waddle
26-Nov-86	L.C. Cup 4	10,033	A	Cambridge United	W 3 - 1 Allen C, Close, Waddle
27-Jan-87	L.C. Cup 5	28,648	A	West Ham United	D 1 - 1 Allen C
02-Feb-87	L.C. Cup 5®	41,995	H	West Ham United	W 5 - 0 Allen C (3, 1pen), Hoddle, Claesen
08-Feb-87	L.C. Cup SF (1)	41,256	A	Arsenal	W 1 - 0 Allen C
01-Mar-87	L.C. Cup SF (2)	37,099	H	Arsenal	L 1 - 2 Allen C
04-Mar-87	L.C. Cup SF	41,005	H	Arsenal	L 1 - 2 Allen C

Tottenham Hotspur - Friendly Matches - Season 1986-1987

| 02-Aug-86 | Friendly/Test | H | Glasgow Rangers | - | D 1 - 1 | Allen C |

Paul Miller Testimonial

04-Aug-86	Friendly	A	Aldershot	-	W 3 - 2	Allen C (2), Galvin
08-Aug-86	Friendly	A	Brighton & HA	-	W 4 - 0	Falco (2), Waddle (2, 1pen)
12-Aug-86	Friendly	A	Gillingham	-	D 1 - 1	Falco
19-Aug-86	Friendly	N	PSV Eindhoven	-	D 1 - 1	Falco

Spurs lost 3-4 on penalties (Scorers: Gough, Stevens, Waddle)

20-Aug-86	Friendly	N	AC Milan	-	W 2 - 1	Falco, Mabbutt
04-Nov-86	Friendly	H	SV Hamburg	-	W 5 - 1	Mabbutt, Allen C (3), Claesen
16-Dec-86	Friendly	A	Bermuda National XI	-	W 3 - 1	Allen C, Hoddle, Waddle (pen)
20-Jan-87	Friendly	A	Linfield	-	W 3 - 2	Allen C (pen), Thomas, og
28-May-87	Friendly	N	Millionaros Columbia	-	L 0 - 1	

235

1987 – 1988 – Manager David Pleat / Terry Venables

Season 1987-1988	Played	Won	Drew	Lost	For	Agst.	Points
Division 1 - 13th	40	12	11	17	38	48	47
F.A. Cup	2	1	0	1	5	3	4th Rnd
League Cup	3	1	0	2	4	3	3rd Rnd
Total - Season 1987-1988	45	14	11	20	47	54	13th

Tottenham Hotspur in the League - Season 1987-1988

15-Aug-87	Division 1	23,947	A	Coventry City	L 1 - 2	Mabbutt
19-Aug-87	Division 1	26,261	H	Newcastle United	W 3 - 1	Allen C, Waddle, Hodge
22-Aug-87	Division 1	37,079	H	Chelsea	W 1 - 0	Claesen
29-Aug-87	Division 1	19,073	A	Watford	D 1 - 1	Allen C (pen)
01-Sep-87	Division 1	21,811	H	Oxford United	W 3 - 0	Allen C, Claesen (2)
05-Sep-87	Division 1	32,389	A	Everton	D 0 - 0	
12-Sep-87	Division 1	24,728	H	Southampton	W 2 - 1	Allen C (pen), Claesen
19-Sep-87	Division 1	27,750	A	West Ham United	W 1 - 0	Fairclough
26-Sep-87	Division 1	47,601	A	Manchester United	L 0 - 1	
03-Oct-87	Division 1	24,311	H	Sheffield Wednesday	W 2 - 0	Allen P, Claesen
10-Oct-87	Division 1	18,669	A	Norwich City	L 1 - 2	Claesen
18-Oct-87	Division 1	36,680	H	Arsenal	L 1 - 2	Claesen
24-Oct-87	Division 1	23,543	A	Nottingham Forest	L 0 - 3	

236

Date	Competition	Attendance	Venue	Opponent	Result	Score	Scorers
31-Oct-87	Division 1	22,282	H	Wimbledon	L	0 - 3	
04-Nov-87	Division 1	15,302	A	Portsmouth	D	0 - 0	
14-Nov-87	Division 1	28,113	H	Queens Park Rangers	D	1 - 1	Allen P
21-Nov-87	Division 1	10,091	A	Luton Town	L	0 - 2	
28-Nov-87	Division 1	47,362	H	Liverpool	L	0 - 2	
13-Dec-87	Division 1	20,392	H	Charlton Athletic	L	0 - 1	
20-Dec-87	Division 1	17,593	A	Derby County	W	2 - 1	Allen C, Claesen
26-Dec-87	Division 1	18,456	A	Southampton	L	1 - 2	Fairclough
28-Dec-87	Division 1	39,456	H	West Ham United	W	2 - 1	Fairclough, Waddle
01-Jan-88	Division 1	25,235	H	Watford	W	2 - 1	Allen C, Moran
02-Jan-88	Division 1	29,317	A	Chelsea	D	0 - 0	
16-Jan-88	Division 1	25,650	H	Coventry City	D	2 - 2	Allen C (2)
23-Jan-88	Division 1	24,616	A	Newcastle United	L	0 - 2	
13-Feb-88	Division 1	9,906	A	Oxford United	D	0 - 0	
23-Feb-88	Division 1	25,731	H	Manchester United	D	1 - 1	Allen C
27-Feb-88	Division 1	18,046	A	Sheffield Wednesday	W	3 - 0	Allen C, Allen P, Claesen
01-Mar-88	Division 1	15,986	H	Derby County	D	0 - 0	
06-Mar-88	Division 1	37,143	A	Arsenal	L	1 - 2	Allen C
09-Mar-88	Division 1	18,662	H	Everton	W	2 - 1	Fairclough, Walsh
12-Mar-88	Division 1	19,322	H	Norwich City	L	1 - 3	Claesen
19-Mar-88	Division 1	8,616	A	Wimbledon	L	0 - 3	
26-Mar-88	Division 1	25,306	H	Nottingham Forest	D	1 - 1	Foster og

02-Apr-88	Division 1	18,616	H	Portsmouth	L	0 - 1	
04-Apr-88	Division 1	14,738	A	Queens Park Rangers	L	0 - 2	
23-Apr-88	Division 1	44,798	A	Liverpool	L	0 - 1	
02-May-88	Division 1	13,977	A	Charlton Athletic	D	1 - 1	Hodge
04-May-88	Division 1	15,437	H	Luton Town	W	2 - 1	Mabbutt, Hodge

Tottenham Hotspur in the FA Cup - Season 1987-1988

| 09-Jan-88 | F.A. Cup 3 | 16,931 | A | Oldham Athletic | W | 4 - 2 | Thomas, Allen C (2), Waddle |
| 30-Jan-88 | F.A. Cup 4 | 20,045 | A | Port Vale | L | 1 - 2 | Ruddock |

Tottenham Hotspur in the League Cup - Season 1987-1988

23-Sep-87	L.C. Cup 2 (1L)	5,000	A	Torquay United	L	0 - 1	
07-Oct-87	L.C. Cup 2 (2L)	20,970	H	Torquay United	W	3 - 0	Claesen (2), Close
28-Oct-87	L.C. Cup 3	29,114	A	Aston Villa	L	1 - 2	Ardiles

238

Tottenham Hotspur - Friendly Matches - Season 1987-1988

23-Jul-87	Friendly	- A Exeter City	W 1 - 0 Metgod
25-Jul-87	Friendly	- A AFC Bournemouth	D 4 - 4 Waddle, Hodge, Allen C (2)
10-Aug-87	Friendly/Test	H Arsenal	W 3 - 1 Thomas, Allen C, Claesen

Chris Hughton Testimonial

20-Oct-87	Friendly/Test	H West Ham United	D 2 - 2 Allen P, Archibald

Tony Galvin Testimonial

10-Nov-87	Friendly	- A St Albans City	W 6 - 0 Samways, Close (2), Howells, Stevens, Stimson
05-Dec-87	Friendly	- A Brentford	D 0 - 0
15-Feb-88	Friendly	- H AS Monaco	L 0 - 4
19-Feb-88	Friendly	- A West Bromwich Albion	L 1 - 4 Walsh
28-Mar-88	Friendly/Test	- H Manchester United	L 2 - 3 Archibald, Hodge

Danny Thomas Benefit match

15-Apr-88	Friendly	- A Hull City	L 1 - 2 Walsh
26-Apr-88	Friendly	- A Crystal Palace	D 3 - 3 Hodge, Walsh, Claesen
06-May-88	Friendly	- A Barnet	W 2 - 1 Waddle (pen), Walsh
10-May-88	Friendly	- A Euskadi Bilbao	L 0 - 4

239

Tottenham Hotspur Tour - Sweden & Finland - Summer 1987

30-Jul-87 Tour	- A Orebro	L 1 - 3 Mabbutt
01-Aug-87 Tour	- A Lansi Uudenmaan Dist	W 7 - 1 Fairclough, Allen C (2), Close (4)
03-Aug-87 Tour	- A IFK/VSK Vasteras XI	W 4 - 2 Waddle, Allen C, Close (2)
05-Aug-87 Tour	- A Marsta IK	W 5 - 0 Claesen (2), Metgod, Mabbutt, Stevens
06-Aug-87 Tour	- A Swedish Div1N Select XI	L 0 - 1

1988 – 1989 – Manager Terry Venables

Season 1988-1989	Played	Won	Drew	Lost	For	Agst.	Points
Division 1 - 6th	38	15	12	11	60	46	57
F.A. Cup	1	0	0	1	0	1	3rd Rnd
League Cup	5	2	2	1	6	5	4th Rnd
Total - Season 1988-1989	44	17	14	13	66	52	6th

Tottenham Hotspur in the League - Season 1988-1989

03-Sep-88	Division 1	32,977	A	Newcastle United	D 2 - 2 Fenwick, Waddle
10-Sep-88	Division 1	32,621	H	Arsenal	L 2 - 3 Gascoigne, Waddle
17-Sep-88	Division 1	40,929	A	Liverpool	D 1 - 1 Fenwick
24-Sep-88	Division 1	23,427	H	Middlesbrough	W 3 - 2 Fenwick (pen), Waddle, Howells
01-Oct-88	Division 1	29,318	H	Manchester United	D 2 - 2 Walsh, Waddle
08-Oct-88	Division 1	14,384	A	Charlton Athletic	D 2 - 2 Fenwick (pen), Allen
22-Oct-88	Division 1	20,330	A	Norwich City	L 1 - 3 Fairclough
25-Oct-88	Division 1	19,517	H	Southampton	L 1 - 2 Ray Wallace og
29-Oct-88	Division 1	26,238	A	Aston Villa	L 1 - 2 Fenwick (pen)
05-Nov-88	Division 1	22,868	H	Derby County	L 1 - 3 Stewart
12-Nov-88	Division 1	23,589	H	Wimbledon	W 3 - 2 Butters, Fenwick (pen), Samways
20-Nov-88	Division 1	15,386	A	Sheffield Wednesday	W 2 - 0 Stewart (2)
23-Nov-88	Division 1	21,961	H	Coventry City	D 1 - 1 Stewart

241

Date		League		Venue	Opponent	Result	Scorers
26-Nov-88	Division 1	26,698	H	Queens Park Rangers	D 2 - 2	Gascoigne, Waddle
03-Dec-88	Division 1	29,657	A	Everton	L 0 - 1	
10-Dec-88	Division 1	27,660	H	Millwall	W 2 - 0	Gascoigne, Waddle
17-Dec-88	Division 1	28,365	A	West Ham United	W 2 - 0	Thomas, Mabbutt
26-Dec-88	Division 1	27,337	H	Luton Town	D 0 - 0	
31-Dec-88	Division 1	27,739	H	Newcastle United	W 2 - 0	Walsh, Waddle
02-Jan-89	Division 1	45,129	A	Arsenal	L 0 - 2	
15-Jan-89	Division 1	16,903	H	Nottingham Forest	L 1 - 2	Waddle
21-Jan-89	Division 1	23,692	A	Middlesbrough	D 2 - 2	Stewart (2)
05-Feb-89	Division 1	41,423	A	Manchester United	L 0 - 1	
11-Feb-89	Division 1	22,803	H	Charlton Athletic	D 1 - 1	Stewart
21-Feb-89	Division 1	19,120	H	Norwich City	W 2 - 1	Gascoigne, Waddle
25-Feb-89	Division 1	16,702	A	Southampton	W 2 - 0	Nayim, Waddle
01-Mar-89	Division 1	19,090	H	Aston Villa	W 2 - 0	Waddle (2)
11-Mar-89	Division 1	18,206	A	Derby County	D 1 - 1	Gascoigne
18-Mar-89	Division 1	17,156	A	Coventry City	D 1 - 1	Waddle
22-Mar-89	Division 1	23,098	A	Nottingham Forest	W 2 - 1	Howells, Samways
26-Mar-89	Division 1	30,012	H	Liverpool	L 1 - 2	Fenwick (pen)
28-Mar-89	Division 1	11,146	A	Luton Town	W 3 - 1	Howells, Walsh, Gascoigne
01-Apr-89	Division 1	28,375	H	West Ham United	W 3 - 0	Fenwick (pen), Nayim, Stewart
12-Apr-89	Division 1	17,270	H	Sheffield Wednesday	D 0 - 0	
15-Apr-89	Division 1	12,366	A	Wimbledon	W 2 - 1	Waddle, Stewart

22-Apr-89	Division 1		28,568	H	Everton	W 2 - 1 Walsh (2)
29-Apr-89	Division 1		16,551	A	Millwall	W 5 - 0 Walsh, Stewart (3), Samways
13-May-89	Division 1		21,873	A	Queens Park Rangers	L 0 - 1

Tottenham Hotspur in the FA Cup - Season 1988-1989

| 09-Jan-89 | F.A. Cup 3 | | 15,917 | A | Bradford City | L 0 - 1 |

Tottenham Hotspur in the League Cup - Season 1988-1989

27-Sep-88	L.C. Cup 2 (1L)	9,269	A	Notts County	D 1 - 1 Samways
11-Oct-88	L.C. Cup 2 (2L)	14,953	H	Notts County	W 2 - 1 Fenwick (pen), Gascoigne
01-Nov-88	L.C. Cup 3	18,814	H	Blackburn Rovers	D 0 - 0
09-Nov-88	L.C. Cup 3	12,961	A	Blackburn Rovers	W 2 - 1 (a.e.t) Thomas, Stewart
29-Nov-88	L.C. Cup 4	17,357	A	Southampton	L 1 - 2 Osman og

Tottenham Hotspur - Friendly Matches - Season 1988-1989

Date			Venue	Opponent	Result	Scorers
07-Aug-88	Friendly	-	A	Dundee United	D 1 - 1	Walsh
10-Aug-88	Friendly	-	A	Reading	L 1 - 2	Gascoigne
13-Aug-88	Friendly	-	W	Arsenal	L 0 - 4	
14-Aug-88	Friendly	-	W	AC Milan	L 1 - 2	Fenwick
16-Aug-88	Friendly	-	A	Chelsea	D 0 - 0	
21-Aug-88	Friendly	-	A	West Ham United	L 0 - 2	
06-Sep-88	Friendly	-	A	Swansea City	W 3 - 0	Gascoigne, Howells, D., Gray
18-Oct-88	Friendly	-	A	Home Farm	W 4 - 0	Own goal, Howells, D., Fenwick, Stewart
17-Jan-89	Friendly	-	H	AS Monaco	L 1 - 3	Moncur (pen)
18-Feb-89	Friendly	Chase L	H	IFK Gothenburg	W 3 - 0	Nayim, Walsh, Robson
04-Mar-89	Friendly	-	H	Bordeaux	L 1 - 2	Mabbutt
04-Apr-89	Friendly	-	A	Charlton Athletic	L 3 - 4	Walsh, Stewart (2)

Tottenham Hotspur Tour - Sweden - Summer 1988

Date			Venue	Opponent	Result	Scorers
26-Jul-88	Tour	-	A	Vederslov/Danningelanda	W 4 - 1	Walsh (3), Stewart (pen)
28-Jul-88	Tour	-	A	Trelleborgs FF	W 3 - 0	Fenwick (2, 1 pen), Moran
31-Jul-88	Tour	-	A	GAIS	D 1 - 1	Walsh
02-Aug-88	Tour	-	A	Jonkoppings Sodra IF	D 1 - 1	Waddle

244

1989 – 1990 – Manager Terry Venables

Season 1989-1990	Played	Won	Drew	Lost	For	Agst.	Points
Division 1 – 3rd	38	19	6	13	59	47	63
F.A. Cup	1	0	0	1	1	3	3rd Rnd
League Cup	6	3	1	2	14	8	5th Rnd
Total - Season 1989-1990	45	22	7	16	74	58	3rd

Tottenham Hotspur in the League - Season 1989-1990

19-Aug-89	Division 1	17,665	H	Luton Town	W 2 - 1	Stewart, Allen
22-Aug-89	Division 1	34,402	A	Everton	L 1 - 2	Allen
28-Aug-89	Division 1	32,004	A	Manchester City	D 1 - 1	Gascoigne
09-Sep-89	Division 1	24,769	A	Aston Villa	L 0 - 2	
16-Sep-89	Division 1	16,260	H	Chelsea	L 1 - 4	Gascoigne
23-Sep-89	Division 1	20,095	A	Norwich City	D 2 - 2	Gascoigne, Lineker
30-Sep-89	Division 1	23,781	H	Queens Park Rangers	W 3 - 2	Lineker (3)
14-Oct-89	Division 1	17,672	A	Charlton Athletic	W 3 - 1	Gascoigne, Lineker, Thomas
18-Oct-89	Division 1	33,944	H	Arsenal	W 2 - 1	Walsh, Samways
21-Oct-89	Division 1	26,909	H	Sheffield Wednesday	W 3 - 0	Lineker (2), Moran
29-Oct-89	Division 1	26,550	A	Liverpool	L 0 - 1	
04-Nov-89	Division 1	19,601	A	Southampton	D 1 - 1	Gascoigne

245

Date	Division	Attendance	H/A	Opponent	Result	Scorers
11-Nov-89	Division 1	26,876	H	Wimbledon	L 0 - 1	
18-Nov-89	Division 1	26,366	A	Crystal Palace	W 3 - 2	Howells, Samways, Lineker (pen)
25-Nov-89	Division 1	28,075	H	Derby County	L 1 - 2	Stewart
02-Dec-89	Division 1	12,620	A	Luton Town	D 0 - 0	
09-Dec-89	Division 1	29,374	H	Everton	W 2 - 1	Stewart, Lineker
16-Dec-89	Division 1	36,230	A	Manchester United	W 1 - 0	Lineker
26-Dec-89	Division 1	26,874	H	Millwall	W 3 - 1	Samways, Lineker, McLeary og
30-Dec-89	Division 1	33,401	H	Nottingham Forest	L 2 - 3	Lineker (2)
01-Jan-90	Division 1	19,599	A	Coventry City	D 0 - 0	
13-Jan-90	Division 1	26,384	H	Manchester City	D 1 - 1	Howells
20-Jan-90	Division 1	46,132	A	Arsenal	L 0 - 1	
04-Feb-90	Division 1	19,599	H	Norwich City	W 4 - 0	Lineker (3, 1pen), Howells
10-Feb-90	Division 1	29,130	A	Chelsea	W 2 - 1	Howells, Lineker
21-Feb-90	Division 1	32,472	H	Aston Villa	L 0 - 2	
24-Feb-90	Division 1	19,676	A	Derby County	L 1 - 2	Moncur
03-Mar-90	Division 1	26,181	H	Crystal Palace	L 0 - 1	
10-Mar-90	Division 1	21,104	H	Charlton Athletic	W 3 - 0	Polston J, Lineker, Howells
17-Mar-90	Division 1	16,691	A	Queens Park Rangers	L 1 - 3	Walsh
21-Mar-90	Division 1	25,656	H	Liverpool	W 1 - 0	Stewart
31-Mar-90	Division 1	26,582	A	Sheffield Wednesday	W 4 - 2	Allen, Lineker (2), Stewart
07-Apr-90	Division 1	21,669	A	Nottingham Forest	W 3 - 1	Stewart, Allen (2)
14-Apr-90	Division 1	23,317	H	Coventry City	W 3 - 2	Lineker (2), Stewart

16-Apr-90	Division 1	10,573	A	Millwall	W 1 - 0 Lineker
21-Apr-90	Division 1	33,317	H	Manchester United	W 2 - 1 Gascoigne, Lineker
28-Apr-90	Division 1	12,800	A	Wimbledon	L 0 - 1
05-May-90	Division 1	31,038	H	Southampton	W 2 - 1 Stewart, Allen

Tottenham Hotspur in the FA Cup - Season 1989-1990

| 06-Jan-90 | F.A. Cup 3 | 33,134 | H | Southampton | L 1 - 3 Howells |

Tottenham Hotspur in the League Cup - Season 1989-1990

20-Sep-89	L.C. Cup 2 (1L)	15,734	H	Southend United	W 1 - 0 Fenwick
04-Oct-89	L.C. Cup 2 (2L)	10,400	A	Southend United	L 2 - 3 (a.e.t) Allen P, Nayim
22-Nov-89	L.C. Cup 3	45,759	A	Manchester United	W 3 - 0 Lineker, Samways, Nayim
22-Nov-89	L.C. Cup 4	13,789	A	Tranmere Rovers	D 2 - 2 Gascoigne, Higgins og
29-Nov-89	L.C. Cup 4	22,720	H	Tranmere Rovers	W 4 - 0 Allen P, Howells, Mabbutt, Stewart
17-Jan-90	L.C. Cup 5	30,044	A	Nottingham Forest	D 2 - 2 Lineker, Sedgeley
24-Jan-90	L.C. Cup 5	32,357	H	Nottingham Forest	L 2 - 3 Nayim, Walsh

Tottenham Hotspur - Friendly Matches - Season 1989-1990

Date	Type	H/A	Opposition	Att	Result	Scorers
19-Jul-89	Friendly	H	Fulham	Chase L	W	3 - 1 Howells (2), Moran
28-Jul-89	Friendly	H	AFC Bournemouth	Chase L	W	6 - 0 Walsh, Stewart, Gascoigne, Howells (3)
01-Aug-89	Friendly	H	Swindon Town	Chase L	L	0 - 1
31-Oct-89	Friendly	A	SM Caen	-	W	2 - 1 Stewart, Howells
06-Nov-89	Friendly	A	Leicester City	-	W	5 - 2 Stewart (2), Gascoigne (2), Sedgley
26-Jan-90	Friendly	A	Plymouth Argyle	-	W	3 - 0 Mabbutt, Gascoigne, og
03-Apr-90	Friendly	A	Brighton & HA	-	W	3 - 0 Gascoigne (2), Stewart
23-Apr-90	Friendly	A	Valerengen	-	D	1 - 1 Howells
01-May-90	Friendly/Test	H	N Ireland XI	6,769	W	2 - 1 Howells, Gascoigne (pen)

Danny Blanchflower Benefit match

Tottenham Hotspur Tour - Ireland, Scotland, Norway & Spain - Summer 1989

Date	Type	H/A	Opposition	Result	Scorers
23-Jul-89	Tour	A	Bohemians	W	2 - 0 Stewart, Walsh
25-Jul-89	Tour	A	Cork City	W	3 - 0 Mabbutt, Gascoigne, Lineker
06-Aug-89	Tour	A	Glasgow Rangers	L	0 - 1
08-Aug-89	Tour	A	Viking	W	5 - 1 Stewart, Fenwick (pen), Gascoigne, Lineker (2)
10-Aug-89	Tour	A	Brann	W	2 - 0 Lineker (2)
11-Aug-89	Tour	A	Dinamo Bucharest	L	1 - 3 Howells
13-Aug-89	Tour	A	Atletico Madrid	L	0 - 1

248

ALSO AVAILABLE FROM THE SAME AUTHOR

'LADS-The Seventies', published in 2008 by Ladsbooks

The first book in the series which follows the Lads on their journey through the violent 1970s. Available now from www.ladsbooks.co.uk

COMING SOON..... 'LADS – THE EUROPEAN TOUR'

More Lads adventures on trips to Holland, Belgium, Spain, Germany, Portugal, the Czech Republic... even Jersey. The story of their hilarious sorties into enemy territories.

ALSO COMING SOON..... 'LADS – THE 90s'

Follow the lads, their scrapes, lives and loves on their journey through the 1990s. Two more Wembley finals. A couple more divorces. Saint Hotspur Day.

'LADS – THE NOUGHTIES'
Planned for publication in 2010 to complete the five book series.

Have you tried these independent Spurs sites? Both are highly recommended...

www.spursodyssey.co.uk Paul Smith's excellent site - "Spurs Odyssey is one of the longest-running established unofficial Spurs sites, featuring a busy message board with unique sources of information, along with nearly 10 years' worth of match reports covering Spurs at all competitive levels". A mine of news and interesting information.

www.topspurs.com "The World Famous (unofficial) home of the Spurs on the web - A website fanzine for the supporters by the supporters". This great site from Jim Duggan includes all THFC results, dates, scorers and attendances since the day dot, as featured in this book.

...Smith, Duggan... I still haven't had my beers from the LAST book!

Lightning Source UK Ltd.
Milton Keynes UK
16 November 2009

146310UK00002B/83/P